T0105031

Getting Out from Under

Getting Out from Under

Leaving Your Business with Your Cash, Sanity, and Soul Intact

Robert J. Fritz

ARCHWAY
PUBLISHING

Copyright © 2014 Robert J. Fritz.

All rights reserved. No part of this book may be used or reproduced by
any means, graphic, electronic, or mechanical, including photocopying,
recording, taping or by any information storage retrieval system
without the written permission of the publisher except in the case
of brief quotations embodied in critical articles and reviews.

The information, ideas, and suggestions in this book are not intended to
render professional advice. Before following any suggestions contained
in this book, you should consult your personal accountant or other
financial advisor. Neither the author nor the publisher shall be liable or
responsible for any loss or damage allegedly arising as a consequence of
your use or application of any information or suggestions in this book.

Archway Publishing books may be ordered through booksellers or by contacting:

Archway Publishing
1663 Liberty Drive
Bloomington, IN 47403
www.archwaypublishing.com
1-(888)-242-5904

Because of the dynamic nature of the Internet, any web addresses or
links contained in this book may have changed since publication and
may no longer be valid. The views expressed in this work are solely those
of the author and do not necessarily reflect the views of the publisher,
and the publisher hereby disclaims any responsibility for them.

Any people depicted in stock imagery provided by Thinkstock are models,
and such images are being used for illustrative purposes only.
Certain stock imagery © Thinkstock.

ISBN: 978-1-4808-0821-8 (sc)
ISBN: 978-1-4808-0822-5 (e)

Library of Congress Control Number: 2014909692

Printed in the United States of America

Archway Publishing rev. date: 06/13/2014

To Linnet

Contents

Introduction

Of the hundreds or thousands of books that have been written about selling your company or creating another exit strategy from your business, almost all have been written by advisors or consultants, not by people who have walked the walk—those who actually have done so. I'm not a professional advisor, but I am a guy who's sold his company. Further, I know a lot of other guys who have been in the same situation.

I've found that the books all talk about the process of exiting and how to maximize your money. While these are obviously important, so are other dimensions. My cash was secure and was more than I would ever need, but I found myself depressed as I contemplated selling my business because I needed a purpose. I also needed to feel like I did some good for all the employees who had helped me get where I was. Accordingly, I wrote a book that discusses all these dimensions of selling a company. I hope you'll find reading it as much fun as I found the challenge of writing it.

Two Kinds of Entrepreneur

There are two distinct types of entrepreneurs. The first starts a family business, which is then usually owned and run by the original founder or by his or her children but rarely survives into a third generation. Many of these founders never intended to start businesses until they came up with good ideas that their employers weren't interested in. After years and years, their businesses became successful. Along the way, the owners tried to maintain low debt—companies of this kind often have zero debt, in fact—because the owners thought debt was bad, and they grew from internally generated funds (profits) instead. Typical owners tie up all of their net worth in shares of their businesses, as usually there are no partners, and if there are, they collectively own less than 51 percent and may be family members or children of the owners.

Many family business are "lifestyle companies," which means that they're businesses for which, at least after a certain point, maximizing the bottom line is not the be-all and end-all for the owners, as it is for the owners of some other companies. The owners of family businesses enjoy the prestige and status of owning a company. They often withdraw less money from the company than they could, and in bad times, they may loan the company money from their personal funds. They sincerely care about employees as people. They may have expensive hobbies, but paradoxically, they're often workaholics and don't like taking vacations because they feel awkward being away from the company and not being in control, even though they know their presence isn't necessary. They're often micromanagers, which can limit the company's size.

Family business owners think of their companies almost as members of their families. They often invest almost all their net worth to start them, even selling their houses in some cases, and have bled for the companies in difficult times to keep them going.

The second type of entrepreneur is the serial entrepreneur. He or she looks at the company only as a source of wealth and piles on as much debt (called leverage) as the company can bear in order to build up the company and sell it for a profit as quickly as possible. Then, he or she may move on to another company and do it again.

My part of the country, northeast Ohio, has a lot of medical startups that work like this: Doctor So-and-So, who has six degrees, invents some device or drug that promises to have medical benefits. He teams up with a serial entrepreneur, who raises funds—equity shares from investors and angel funds, loans from state governments, and the like—to start the business. The serial entrepreneur seldom puts his own money into the venture, though he may take a low salary—$60,000 per year for a year or two, for example—and the doctor keeps his day job. After awhile, the device or pill is made and tested on mice. If these are successful, the entrepreneur goes back and raises more capital for tests on pigs. The idea is to sell the whole company (its only real assets being patents and test results) to a major pharmaceutical company before any of the pills or devices actually are sold on the market. Sometimes this works.

Not all serial entrepreneurs are like this, however. Tony Hseih is an example. This young man was a software genius. He and his friend once spent a weekend writing software that they turned into a company, which they later sold to

Microsoft for $230 million. Tony then took his money and bought into Zappo's, the online shoe store, bringing many new ideas too, and changing the culture for the better.

This book is written mostly for the first type of entrepreneur, the type who has bled for the company and almost thinks of it as one of his or her children, although serial entrepreneurs may learn a thing or two as well. It's founder-owner-operators who put their own skin in the game whom I most admire, but paradoxically, their companies often lose their value. Hopefully this book will tell you how to avoid that.

Why Don't Business Owners Do What Exit Planners Tell Them to Do?

A lot of small or mid-sized business owners are brilliant. At sales or manufacturing, they have no equal. Some of them compete around the edges of big companies such as GE or Honeywell, and my experience has told me that they've got about a fifty-point IQ advantage over the people in these big companies. They've built their own companies, either by growing in their markets or by inventing new markets. Moreover, they've done so without borrowing money. They remember that when they first got started, it was touch-and-go whether they would make payroll on Fridays, and the last thing they want now are bankers interfering with their businesses.

But then they get old. So a whole industry of planners, helpers, lawyers, accountants, investment bankers, brokers, and others has arisen to help them plan their exits from their businesses. The trouble is, most business owners don't *want* to think about exiting.

In 2003 Jeff Babcock spoke at my Vistage[1] group's monthly meeting. He spoke on building the sustainable firm. By "sustainable," he meant that the firm could carry on after the owner-founder-operator left. The audience at the meeting included about fifteen CEOs of small and medium firms, most of whom were also owners of their firms. At the beginning of the presentation, he asked how many of us in the audience had an exit strategy. Not one hand went up. The speaker said that wasn't surprising; he had been giving such presentations for several years and had only found one Vistage CEO who had bothered to think of an exit strategy. Three hours later, at the end of the presentation, the speaker had each of us make up and share an exit strategy with the group. That presentation really woke me up. But besides me, only one other person in the room actually followed his or her exit strategy, at least during the years I kept in touch with them.

Why do business owners avoid exit planning? A lot of them stick with their businesses far too long, riding them down and dying with much less money for their families than they should have had. I believe they do this because they think of the business as part of themselves, like their homes, their families, or their friends. Many of them, in fact, have no real friends outside of the business. So they hang on as long as they can. "I'll plan an exit tomorrow" could describe their attitude.

---

1   Vistage is an association of approximately twelve thousand CEOs, most of them from small or midsized companies, many of whom own their companies. Vistage is organized into groups of approximately 15 CEOs, each group being facilitated by a Vistage "Chair."

Also, you may not realize it, but exiting a small business requires a lot of work, more than leaving almost any other position. You don't own your business; your business owns you. Unlike Jack Welch, the pope, the janitor, or ordinary mortals, you can't just quit. Leaving is a lengthy process.

In other words, exiting your business is almost as difficult as starting it!

For some businesses, especially those that are very small or businesses without stakeholders such as children, families, and key loyal employees, ignoring exit plans seems okay. I knew a guy who collected rare guns as sort of a business. When my father died, I inherited a bunch of rare and antique guns and, knowing something about their values, proceeded to sell them. I found out that this guy, in his sixties, who had no children and no living relatives except his mother and who was in poor health, would buy a lot of what I had. Finally, I asked him why he still did this. After all, he had 350 old guns. What would happen when he died? He said he didn't care. He would be gone and someone else would take care of it.

For most of us, this isn't okay.

Most people smart enough to run businesses know that they have to do some succession planning because they can't live forever. They say "I'll do it later," because worry about sales, production, and the like is more fun, more challenging, and less angst-inducing than worrying about exit planning. So when is *later*?

In addition, most planners and advisors don't understand the inherent conflict business owners face. We don't want to face selling our businesses because they're our lives, and we can't imagine life without them. We're concerned that we'll have to work for years for the new owners, and our very DNA doesn't want us to work for anyone. Or we think, *I don't need to plan because when the business is ready, a buyer will find me.* The buyer will not find you when you're ready, although the other excuses are basically true.

What it comes down to is that you already have an exit strategy. It's called dying. It will disrupt the business and your family. So what do you want to do with the remaining years of your life?

Do you want to be king, or do you want to be rich?

Do You Want to Be King, or Do You Want to Be Rich?

If you own and run a successful company, you know what it's like to be king. You come to work at 8:00 in the morning. The young lady nods and smiles at you as you pass by to go to your office, the best corner office in the place. You hang up your coat in the closet and then go out to the coffee machine, greeting any office employees you come across. Then you decide to walk around the plant, making mental notes about progress on products or maintenance needs. Hourly workers greet you and smile. Like at most companies, they don't belong to labor unions.

Returning to your office, you leave the door open. The sales manager walks in to discuss a problem he's discovered. Like all your direct reports do for all such problems, he states the problem and then suggests a solution before you discuss it. You smile when you think about how hard it's been to persuade the sales force that they're not allowed to lose orders because of price, but they are allowed to tell you they're *going* to lose an order because of price. Then you tell the sales manager what to do.

You next check your schedule on the computer. The mayor is coming at 10:00 a.m.; it's just a social call. The mayor likes businesses to be happy in his town, a suburb of a major city, and you represent one of the ten largest employers there.

At noon, you've been asked to have lunch with important customers from Asia. It's always important for them to meet the company president.

After lunch, the contractor arrives with the architect to review plans for the new plant you're considering. It's expensive as you-know-what. You're very conservative, but when you do the math, you see it will be hard to lose money on this deal. Your company has zero debt right now, unlike in earlier years when you wondered if customer payments would arrive in time for Friday's payroll. Your bank keeps trying to lend you money, but you prefer to keep a large cash reserve for any difficulties that arise.

You will leave early today, an unusual occurrence. You have to attend a board meeting at your grandchildren's private school, as you're a respected member of this board, along with several others, and your company makes an annual contribution to the school.

After dinner, you go to a meeting of your church council. The other members look at you with a little awe—and jealousy. They are a high school football coach, a plumbing contractor, a post-office employee, and the like. Your car is more expensive, newer, and cleaner than theirs are. You also seem to know more about running an enterprise, including the church.

That's what it's like to be king, at least the good parts. Owning a small or medium-sized business makes you freer than practically anyone else in the history of the planet. It's like being king of a small country in the Middle Ages, except you have no fear that the Ottoman Turks will violate the rules and come in to kill everybody. Instead, the US government makes the rules, and they are predictable. No Ottomans. You're also far freer than the CEO of a large company, as you have no boards or other constituents to worry about. If you've treated people reasonably fairly, you'll have no dysfunctional labor unions stirring up trouble. You don't have to spend a month each year making charts with squiggly lines to communicate with boards or shareholders. You are free.

You're free, that is, as long as you stay king. But if you decide to abdicate, you'll find that you're a little less free than you thought. The president of GE can just quit. That's unlikely, but it was unlikely that the pope would quit. Yet the pope did just that with barely a month's notice. You as king can't do that very well. You'll find it will take a couple of years for you to abdicate, which we'll discuss later, and I think that's why some of us don't want to quit being king. Unfortunately, we all have to abdicate, and if we don't plan for it, we'll get sick and die or have a stroke, and then our abdication will not allow our families to have serene retirements. It's always best to abdicate before you have to, as Czar Nicholas of Russia learned in 1917.

So as king, you get to remain free, for now. But in the long term, you don't own your business: your business owns you.

In the meantime, about the only disadvantage of your position, assuming you take reasonable care to manage it well, is that you're not really rich in a discretionary sense. Sure, your wealth is measured in millions of dollars, and sure, you probably have more material things than any of your high school friends—a big house and condo in some warm place with no mortgages—and your grandchildren's college tuition is already paid for. But your *real* wealth is tied up in your business. It's what we call *illiquid*. So you can't spend it, and you're not rich. In addition, you may have other encumbrances such as other owners of the business.

So what would it be like to sell the company like your hordes of advisors and planners recommend and be rich?

Well, in the first place, you probably wouldn't have any financial worries. You would sit in an office in your basement. No one would come to see you, and few would call. You would go from being a minor potentate to being lonely. People would approach you with "investment opportunities" that invariably consist of your investing a lot of money in some venture for a minority share. They want your money, not your skills. After you invest the money, they want you to sit down and shut up! You would become a financial morphine drip, nothing more. If things worked out, years later, you would get a return on your investment, but that would mean very little to you.

After successfully selling your business, you may have more freedom than you've ever known. But freedom does not necessarily equal happiness.

And that's why many—or even most—business owners fear selling their businesses. The advisors and planners can't really understand. It's inconceivable to them that a person could ever have enough money, so they don't understand why more money wouldn't make you happy. They forget the lesson of Maslow's hierarchy of needs: As Maslow wrote in1943, a satisfied need ceases to motivate. This is especially true for highly competitive business owners.

I think that most of us would rather be king than rich, as the terms are used here. This is the reason why people who own businesses are unwilling to sell or otherwise exit them. Since much of the literature written for us talks about how to maximize our wealth, it misses a lot of the target audience's concerns.

Many advisors will tell you to become passionate about hobbies in preparation for your exit because after you exit, they say, you'll have to find something to work hard at. Well, this is true, but unfortunately, it runs counter to business people's nature. Most successful businesspeople, especially those who start or own companies, are very driven people. They are not sitting around saying, "If only I had time to play golf every day." It's hard to transition from being king to playing golf every day.

I well remember reading a book called *Genghis Kahn: Emperor of All Men*, written in 1926 by Harold Lamb that, amazingly enough, has a lot of lessons for running and owning a business today. One day, the great Kahn, who ruled an empire larger than any that existed before or since, asked one of his officers what, in all the world, could bring the greatest happiness. 'The open steppe, a clear day, and a swift horse,' responded the officer, 'and a falcon on your wrist to start up hares.' 'Nay,' replied the Khan. 'To crush your enemies. That is best.'[2]

The Khan would not have responded well to advice to enjoy hobbies. His only hobby was his "business." Many of us are like that. We work not to have time for golf or fancy cars or big houses, we work to work. We would rather be king than be rich, and that is why the thought of selling our businesses is hard to think about.

So what can you do to transition from being king to being rich without feeling like a has-been fool?

Having Your Cake and Eating It Too

Since planning an exit strategy is so painful for most of us, some of us simply put it off. This is akin to what an alcoholic does when he realizes he is an alcoholic and will have to quit drinking. "I'll quit next week," he says. Business owners, in the interim, can either take out enough money from their companies right now or can step up their withdrawals, thus remaining king and being rich too. The only problem is that their capacities will diminish and they will eventually die, and a long time before that, the value of their companies will decline.

---

2   Harold Lamb, *Genghis Kahn, the Emperor of All Men,* Garden City Publishing Company, 1926. Pg. 107

I like to think of a business as having a finite lifetime, just like its owner. This lifetime progresses through five stages. As originally charted by the Falls River Group, these are:

1. Wonder

2. Thunder

3. Plunder

4. Blunder

5. Going under

Stage 3 is where some of us are now, the stage at which owners or founders seek to have their cake and eat it too. The problem is that this can lead to stage 4 and, if businesses don't recover quickly, stage 5.

I was recently briefly involved with a business that manufactured complicated instruments that was blasting through all five stages. It was founded after World War II by several brothers, and over the years, it had grown to about $25 million in sales. Eventually, all the brothers died except for one, who remained as chairman of the board. Members of the family held all the other key management positions and provided an extreme example of stage 3, plunder. Most of them didn't have adequate backgrounds for their jobs, which harmed the company as surely as if they paid out large amounts of cash to each other without reason, and maybe they did. Now, there's nothing wrong with nepotism if the managers are competent, but these weren't. They had degrees and experience unrelated to the industry. The company went from plunder to blunder. Sales dropped in half and profits were negative.

A few years later, the company was in danger of going under. They finally hired someone from outside the family—an experienced manager who actually had relevant industry experience—to fix things. His plan would cost several million dollars, so the company hired an investment banker to gin up the cash, but with no success. I predict this company will either go under or be sold for practically nothing, destroying the family's once considerable wealth.

The root cause of the problem was the family's attempt to hold on to the company after they had lost the ability to run it.

The problem is not how to have your cake and eat it too. The problem is you are eventually going to die.

This means you will not be king anymore, no matter what you do. So the only choice for you and your family may be to be rich, and to be happy being rich.

That's a hard thing for many of us to accept.

This book is about when and how to go from being king to being rich with as few repercussions as possible.

The First Thing

You're going to die, so when should you start planning your business exit strategy? Right now. If you're sixty-four and want to exit when you're sixty-five, start now. If you're forty and want to exit when you're sixty-five, start now. The sooner you do this, the more certainty you'll have, and the happier you'll be. You don't have to *exit* right now, mind you. Just *plan* the exit right now. The following shows the stages of planning my exit strategy, even though I wasn't sure what my exit strategy would be and perhaps wasn't even sure that a particular action was a part of it:

> Fourteen years before exit: Began paying dividends so the stockholders (the family) could have considerable assets outside the firm.
>
> Seven years before exit: Transferred considerable equity to the founder's grandchildren (my children and my sister's children) so that future growth would pass to them without taxes.
>
> Six years before exit: Urged my subordinates to more aggressively increase earnings and value.
>
> Four years before exit: Did a lot of research and

decided on 2005 as the exit time period. Investigated ESOPs, management buyout, borrowing plus cash payout, and sale.

Vince Lombardi said, "Winning isn't the most important thing. Winning is the only thing." I say, "Having a lot of money isn't the most important thing, but it'd better danged well be the first thing."

What that means is that the very first thing to do is to figure out how much money you're going to need. Then you can figure out how to get it.

It's a lot easier than you might think to figure out how much money you need. Most of us are familiar with the 4 percent rule, and I prefer to use a 3 percent rule because it's more conservative. According to this rule, you start with how much money you need annually for the lifestyle you desire. Let's say this is $300,000. Next, if you use the 4 percent rule, you divide that figure by 0.04. The answer is $7.5 million. Using the 3 percent rule, the answer is $10 million. That figure is how much money you need to start with to have an almost perfect chance to maintain your $300,000-a-year standard of living for the rest of your life, allowing for market fluctuations, inflation, and the like.

I have a friend who is even more conservative. He simply says he needs $15 million. This gives him $5 million to squander on a business his kids may want to start, and if it goes bust, he still has the $10 million.

Incidentally, don't worry about where to invest your money at this point. This book doesn't give investment advice anyway.

Lately, financial advisors have begun to question the 4 or 3 percent rule, pointing out that if two or three real down years happen in the market during the first several years, you'll end up with a lot less money than you planned to have due to the mathematics of the "Monte Carlo simulation." You can use several methods to fight this, but all involve moderating your withdrawals or sacrificing your principal to ensure reasonably constant annual income. I have preferred to use 3 percent instead of 4 percent to be conservative and to assume that the financial crisis of 2008 to 2011 was unusual and is unlikely to recur. Sure, my method provides no guarantee of safety, but there's no guarantee that a meteor won't hit your house either.

I call the amount you need to start the *secure threshold value*, or STV. Now you have to get your assets to be worth whatever amount you've computed because when you're at STV or above it, you'll have financial security for the rest of your life. That's the first thing.

Of course, don't forget assets outside of your business when computing the STV. You may have an IRA, other market investments, or real estate beyond your housing needs. Also, don't forget to subtract any debt you have.

A friend started a company and ran it for thirty years before he thought about succession. He had figured out a way to procure waste chemicals from large companies either for next to nothing or for free and turn them into a useful product. He had built the business up to just under $20 million in sales, and although profits were sporadic, the business survived and got bigger. When he was in his mid-sixties, like many of us, he reached out to his advisors, his lawyer, and his accountant and asked their advice. He then came up with an exit plan and presented it to a group of CEO friends for their advice.

The basic idea of the plan fell into the have-my-cake-and-eat-it-too category: he would retire to another state and concentrate on his hobby, and his son would run the company. Each year, his son and his daughters, the latter of whom had nothing to do with the company, would each take out an equal amount of money, and my friend would take out a larger share. Naturally, he could come back for visits and make suggestions.

You can see where this was going. My friend would never relinquish control, though he wouldn't know as much about the business anymore; the son would do most of his work, assuming he got over his great resentment for having to do all the work for only a small take; and the daughters would get something for nothing. This could never work. For one thing, the father needed to get all the way out of the picture. And none of them had calculated how much they needed to take out to support their lifestyles.

My friend started off saying the company was worth $5 million. He had calculated its worth to be five times the EBITDA of the previous year (more about this later). Unfortunately, he'd forgotten that the business had $4 million of debt, so the real value was $1 million. And his accountant forgot about taxes on the sale.

Remember, the value of your company must be reduced by any debt you have but also increased by any subchapter S accumulated and undistributed earnings. And don't forget to calculate the taxes on proceeds. Capital gains taxes—and most of the proceeds will likely be capital gains—were 15 percent in 2012 and are 23.8 percent in 2014. Thank you, Mr. Obama. Also, some states, including Ohio, have no state capital gains tax, so you have to pay state income tax on the proceeds. That's 5.42% percent in Ohio right now.[3]

Back to our example, let's say that the father needed $300,000 of income annually. The son or any other competent president would want about the same. Then we have the daughters. If the company were only worth $1 million, these payouts would hit that limit pretty soon.

What Is Your Company Worth?

This is also surprisingly easy to *approximate*. What you want to figure out is how much it would be worth to an outside buyer, even if you want to have your kids or the current managers own it. How do you do this? A bank at least of regional size will have an officer whose job it is to facilitate mergers and acquisitions. Just ask that officer at your bank.

The officer will start with a figure called EBITDA—earnings before interest, taxes, depreciation, and amortization—or

---

3   Both rates are for the maximum tax bracket as of 2014.

will just take net profit and add in interest, depreciation, and amortization. Then, based on the industry, the size of the company, and the stability of the earnings (whether EBITDA is reasonably constant, increasing year to year, or has fluctuated a lot), the value will be some multiple of EBITDA. As I write this, it is between four times for smaller companies and nine times for larger ones in such favored industries as medical devices. For most privately owned manufacturing companies, it is about five to seven times right now. And don't forget to subtract any debt. I have to emphasize that any such EBITDA multiple is only an approximation, as it depends on the stability of your earnings year over year.

So ask the banker. Don't fall for the glamorous-model syndrome—"Yeah but it's *my* company, so it must be Claudia Schiffer," or worth a lot more than seven times EBITDA.

In my friend's case, suppose he needed $300,000 annually to live on. Using the 4 percent rule, we see that this would require him to receive $7.5 million if he were to sell outright. Forget the children for the time being; they would only get to inherit what he hasn't spent when he dies. The value of his business would be about $1 million, assuming five times EBITDA, because of the debt, and it's probably less than five times because the $1-million EBITDA figure was not very stable year to year, and even less after taxes and selling costs.

What this one example amounted to was that in his sixties, my friend discovered that he did not have enough money to retire. But you don't have to despair about this happening to you. When you're in your fifties or your forties, calculate how much your business has to be worth, the STV, using the 3 or 4 percent rule, and then plan to make it worth that. That will focus you. Once you get above the STV, you've basically got it made financially. You can even afford to make mistakes.

And, by the way, when you calculate what your company is worth, bear in mind that you will not come up with an exactly accurate number. With luck, you'll get within 20 percent of the actual value. When I sold my company, I asked the investment banker what it was worth, and the highest offer I received was 12 percent less than that. Some offers even wanted me to finance 25 percent of the deal. So I took it off the market, and six months later, I sold it for 22 percent more than the investment banker's estimate. Any of these numbers from negative 12 percent to positive 22 percent would probably not have affected my lifestyle afterward, as I realized that it's good to have a cushion by having taken some money out before you start the sale.

And, while I'm throwing around all these numbers, consider that any buyer will only be interested in EBITDA calculated using generally accepted accounting principles—GAAP. My company had its books audited each year by a quality CPA firm to ensure this, but many private companies, especially smaller ones, don't do this. I know of one case in which a company claimed that it earned $1 million, but the GAAP calculation showed it had earned only $600,000.

Making Your Company Worth What It Needs to Be Worth

Suppose my friend in the example from the previous chapter wants to retire on $300,000 a year and let each of his kids have $1 million cash. Right now, remember, the company *might* be worth $1 million. Instead, my friend needs it to be worth $5 million for his kids and, using the 4 percent rule, $7.5 million for himself. That's $12.5 million total, after capital gains taxes on the sale, for the secure threshold value (STV). To include capital gains and state taxes, he might consider he needs to sell it for about $17 million. How does he get from here to there starting in his sixties?

The answer, probably, is he doesn't! That's why you should start your estate and exit planning as early as possible.

In the example, for the transition to work at all, the father would have to have some assets outside the company. If he didn't, he would be reluctant to give up any control. Although he would retire to Florida, every time there was a twitter in the business, he would rush back to the company to take charge, and he'd likely foul it up worse because he hadn't been there and didn't know what was going on. His son would resent his intervention, or if the son were only nominally president of the company, the daughters would resent it. The strife could crater the company and the family. And it just may be that they would never get to their STV. After all, most working people who don't own businesses don't get there.

This would be the right way for the father to exit:

1. The father builds up substantial assets *outside* the company.

2. The father sells the company to the children. How? The company is recapitalized into voting and non-voting shares, with the non-voting shares having most of the value. These shares, or a portion of them, are sold to the children in exchange for notes to pay for them over time. Because the business has two classes of stock, he can do this and maintain control. The repayment of the notes is based on an appraisal of the company's worth and what the company can afford to pay out in dividends each year. As noted, my method of EBITDA estimation is only for planning purposes. An outside audit is necessary to satisfy the IRS.

3. Each year, the company pays dividends to the stockholders (the children and any others), who immediately pay back the father. The children never see the cash until the note is paid off.

4. The son is allowed buy more of the company than his sisters, since he's going to work in it and run it. "Oh, golly!" you might say. "You mean the division of assets isn't exactly equal?" That's exactly what I mean. Equal and fair are not necessarily the same. However, the daughters should have a buy/sell agreement that gives them the right to sell their stock to their brother, by some equitable formula and over a specified time.

5. The father ends up with a yearly income, of course, and also has some assets as a cushion.

This plan might have a fighting chance of working, although the parties would find it difficult to reach their $12.5-million STV. However, the father would get a comfortable retirement, the son would get to be majority owner of a good company, assuming he could grow and run it, and the daughters would get a smaller share of the proceeds. The daughters should also probably get a larger share of the father's non-business assets in his estate.

Had the family started twenty years before they did, they might have had a chance to make the STV larger. Since they didn't, at least the father could have leveled with his kids so they knew they wouldn't inherit so much money that they wouldn't have to make their own careers.

Start Even Earlier

I knew of a company started by a guy with three sons who decided when he exited that the fairest option would be to give equal shares to each of his sons. Eventually, after the father's exit and death, the company grew to have six hundred employees and was quite valuable.

What about the three sons?

The first son, my friend, ran the company. He had created most of its growth and value.

The second son moved to another state, started his own company, and became a businessman and a millionaire.

The third son was a motorcycle bum. He had no means of support except freebie dividends from the company and often no permanent address. At the age of fifty-four, he had a child out of wedlock with some hippie chick.

At this point, the company president thought it would be a very good idea to buy out his brothers, and he figured out a fair and lucrative offer. The second brother understood it immediately and agreed. But the third brother complained that he didn't have time to fool with all that legal stuff, didn't want to read or sign anything, and only wanted to ride his motorcycle.

A disaster was averted only after much negotiation. The third brother did eventually sell, but can you imagine what would have happened if the hippie chick had left the motorcycle guy and the motorcycle guy died? There would have been a heck of a lawsuit on behalf of the kid.

Here's another example: A man who was an alcoholic started a company. He had two sons, one of whom was not an alcoholic and was very responsible, and one who was an alcoholic. The founder's will divided the company equally between the sons. The nonalcoholic son was president and worked to grow the company. The alcoholic son had a key position but missed lots of work because of his drinking. You can imagine what would happen when the father passed away.

The point of all this? Equality is not good. It's not the same as fairness. If a founder has more than one child, one of them is going to be more competent to run the company than the others. So, if you're thinking of leaving the company to the kids, make sure that one of them owns it. Compensate the others in some other way.

If you're the child of the founder—and many of us are nowadays because of so many businesses were founded in the decades after World War II—you must insist that the interests of all siblings be settled up front, and that all understand the plans. Don't wait for some future event to provide resolution. What would have happened if my friend, one of three brothers, when informed that the company was going to be divided equally, had insisted on some buyout clause before his father's passing? What would happen to my other friend with the alcoholic brother after their father died? Even worse, what would happen if his alcoholic brother died and left his entire estate to his wife who got remarried? Things like this are why so many family businesses devolve into basic warfare. Resolve conflicts early, and don't leave room for contingencies.

Then there's my situation. My father founded the company. I had a good career in a similar business and was advancing, but my father sustained an injury, and our family lawyer convinced me that if I didn't come back to the family business, it might go under. My father said he would work something out so I could buy all the stock, and I came back at age twenty-eight. This was my first mistake. I should have insisted on a contract to buy the stock before I came back. But I made the business grow, and my father, to his credit, mostly stayed out of the way. After awhile he made a job for my sister, and although she tried very hard and was smart, her background and experience was less important to the company than mine, in my opinion.

One Christmas my father gave my sister and me each some shares of the company. Later, the company grew more. When I was about forty, my father announced his succession plan. My sister and I would each inherit 50 percent of the stock. However, a small portion of each of our shares would be set aside in a special pool that I controlled as long as I was alive and sound. Otherwise, my sister would control it. In effect, I would control the company during my life. Mistake number two: I didn't think anything of this. I should have insisted that I or my side of the family retain permanent control.

Years passed, my father passed away, and I continued to make the company grow. Finally—more about this later—I decided to sell the company and, thankfully, was able to convince my sister to help me do this. Among my reasons for selling was that I feared my sister would run the company into the ground if I died, destroying my family's wealth. My sister became very wealthy from the proceeds of her share of the company, which I thought she might not have earned, but I didn't begrudge her this. I had earned it for her.

The new owners kept me around and paid me for two and a half years but fired her. That created unbelievable strife, with my sister claiming that our father had intended each of us to have exactly half, that she was getting cheated, that I should pay her husband's medical bills, and so on. For a couple of years we barely spoke to each other. That was not what my father had intended when he set up the succession plan.

Finally, if you have any remaining doubt that equal is not the same as fair, consider another friend of mine who related this story about his father: The father and a partner started a business that made bubble-pack displays, the things you see on tabs in hardware stores containing a few picture hangers or other small items.

The father and his partner each owned exactly 50 percent. They were very compatible, and the business prospered for twenty years or so. They saw no need for a succession plan, thinking that each one's will and estate documents would let his heirs inherit his share and that things would go on the same as always. Alarm bells and sirens should have gone off!

Finally, one of the partners died. The deceased partner's wife remarried, and her new husband had entirely different ideas about how to run the company. By this time the surviving partner was in his seventies, and there was much acrimony between him and the new husband. This finally degenerated into lawsuits, and the business suffered as a result. At a critical point, a flood destroyed much of the plant, and it was found that someone had neglected to renew the insurance. Each side blamed the other. More lawsuits. Eventually a judge invoked a little-known state law and told both parties that if they did not come to an agreement about dividing the assets within one month, the judge would sell them individually to the highest bidder. Both sides lost.

How to Do It Right

I know a guy who started an industrial distributorship shortly after World War II. He had three children. One child had the background and ability to succeed in running such a company, but the others did not, so the father arranged for the first child to buy the company. The second child got the real estate the company used in its business and the rents it generated. The third child got some other assets outside the business. After many years, the first son built the business to over $100 million of revenue. Its value was clearly more than what the other two kids got. But he had built it with his own hard work. Equal? No. Fair? Yes.

So here's the takeaway: If you have a company and are considering your kids' taking it over, do *not* give them equal shares of your company. Instead, figure out which one should have controlling interest. If you are one of the kids, do *not* blithely smile and say nothing when your parent announces an exit, leaving any rough edges to be resolved later. Instead, insist they be resolved *now*.

After that, you can make an exit strategy. Then the real fun begins.

What to Do with It Part I: Keep It in the Family?

I think that most of us would like to see our children follow in our footsteps and take over our businesses. But before we can even consider this, we must ask ourselves three questions:

1. Is he or she competent to run the business? Here's where Claudia Schiffer syndrome can really set in. Your child just may not be Claudia Schiffer, or as smart as you were or as interested as you were or as lucky as you or as sociable as you ...

2. Does he or she want to run it? A lot of kids are forced into following in their parents' footsteps instead of choosing their own path.

3. What about jealousies within the family? Remember, you *must* arrange for one child to be the boss and majority owner. Will this cause so much strife that you'd be better off selling and splitting up the money?

Consider your kids rationally. Do they have the right degrees to run your business? Depending on your business, this might be a technical degree or maybe an MBA. Was their class standing in the upper 25 percent? What leadership positions, including in clubs and school organizations, have they achieved? Do they like to sell? What other jobs (and there should be some) have they had? Were they promoted or positively evaluated at those jobs? Have these involved skills necessary for your business? What do they read in their spare time? Who are their friends?

Make your own list of questions, one perhaps twice as long as this. If you stumble or find yourself making rationalizations as you go through it, perhaps your kids shouldn't run the business. Your biggest problem will be looking at your kids *objectively*. Most of us have a hard time doing this.

Caution: also consider how adaptable your kid is. A professional engineer with twelve patents and a company employing graduate engineers might have a kid with a BA in finance. But is the kid able to hire or appoint a technical lieutenant? Or is it necessary for the owner to understand the products technically as much as it was when the company was started? But don't look at this kid with rose-colored glasses. What in the kid's prior work experience indicates that he or she can actually do this?

As an extreme case, I know of a man who decided his son should become governor or at least a high-ranking official of his state. The father was a responsible citizen and had held management jobs in state government most of his life. He continuously pressured his son into situations the son could not cope with. The son was thrown out of a prep school and developed a drug habit in high school, but the father ignored it. The son barely graduated from college and then barely graduated from a third-rate law school. He flunked the bar exam three times. After holding a number of intern-type jobs with state and local government, he and his girlfriend, who had twice served time for selling illegal drugs, moved in with his parents. The girlfriend robbed the parents blind, taking everything including the mother's jewelry and, using his debit card number, money from the father's checking account.

While this was going on, the son finally passed the bar exam and was struggling to make $6,000 per year as a lawyer. He received a DUI, was arrested for cocaine and heroin possession, and was subsequently convicted for attempting to coerce a prostitute who had changed her mind. His law license was suspended. Yet, the father insisted that his son was one of the best lawyers in the United States and was working on a case that would soon pay him $1.5 million. After the conviction, the only income for father and son was the father's pension and Social Security. Two years after the father passed away, the son, age fifty-six, was told his house would be auctioned off because of nonpayment of taxes. He had no running water, having not paid that bill either. He had no television. He had no telephone and communicated only through e-mail. He had severe medical problems including a grossly swollen foot from diabetes but he could not afford medical help.

So love is blind, not only for members of the opposite sex but within families.

If you do decide to turn your business over to your kids, don't think you can do something simple and easy, like leave it to them in your will. Unless the value is very small, you'll have estate taxes to contend with, and you'll have to retain ownership until you die. If all you have is ownership and no other assets in your STV, you'll continually fret that the kids are screwing the business up. You'll have nightmares about being old and poor. You'll continually interfere, and one day you *will* screw it up. So if you want to turn your business over to your kids, sell it to them at fair market value, at least as much as your STV, and retire. Don't rely on income from your business after turning ownership over to your kids or to anyone else.

This requires starting very early, preferably when you're in your forties. There's a lot of work to do, but your lawyer and accountant are probably pretty good at this sort of thing. If not, get new ones.

First, get the company appraised by a specialized appraiser. Second, sell a lot of the stock to your kids in the way outlined in the next paragraph.

Assuming your kids don't have the cash to buy the business, they give you a note. Then, plan for the company to pay dividends to all stockholders, including you and your children, each year. Your children's dividends will go toward paying off the note. After some years, the note will be paid off, and you'll have some cash and your heirs will have bought a large part of the company at something less than current market value, assuming that it has continued to grow during this time.

When the note is paid off, simply do it again. Eventually the heirs will own most of the company. Of course, before starting, split the stock 100 to 1 or so into nonvoting shares (the majority portion) and voting shares. You keep the voting shares, and you give the heirs a good deal because their stock is nonvoting, is not marketable, and is not the majority of the stock. They can probably buy $100 worth of stock for about $65, if that's what you want, and if you think about it, that's better than giving the residual to the government. The interest they pay you can also be very low—the IRS even has a special low rate for it.

I must emphasize starting early, in this case because it reduces taxes. If you die, your kids will owe inheritance taxes. If you give away or sell the company to your kids a piece at a time, it will be subject to gift-tax discounts for lack of marketability and minority ownership. However, if your kids buy pieces early, they will avoid gift taxes on the subsequent value, assuming it grows, and you can give much of it away while maintaining control.

Again, if anything seems too complex, just ask your lawyer about it. It's really simple to sell your company to your kids. You just have to start about twenty years ahead. And make sure you end up with your STV free and unencumbered outside the company.

If you don't sell the company to your kids, they'll still end up with a lot of money, and if you're at all worried they'll squander it, you can control it through trusts both after the sale and after you're gone.

What to Do with It Part 2: The Management Buyout

A management buyout happens when an owner sells the company to a key manager or, less commonly, a group of managers younger than the owner in most cases. Usually, as time goes on and the owner gets less and less interested in the hassle of running the business, a key manager takes over more and more responsibility. As the owner gets older, becomes more burned out, or both, the manager makes it known that he or she would like to buy the business to initiate the process. Sometimes a management buyout becomes necessary for the continued success of the business.

But here is a major conundrum:

If the owner wants to sell the business to anyone, the prospective buyer will want to have good management intact and will want to meet the key manager. In fact, the key manager will usually have to make presentations to prospective buyers. This will not work if the manager is disgruntled because he or she has been denied an opportunity to buy the business.

An equally bad problem for morale can arise if the employees respect the manager, hope that he or she buys the company, and then find out that the owner won't sell to him or her.

So why not just sell the company to the key manager? The problem is that in general, such a manager doesn't have enough money to buy it at all or will only be able to buy it for less than a third party would, and the owner will most likely have to finance a portion of the sale. On the other hand, the management buyout process is very easy and avoids most of the hassle associated with a third-party sale.

Here is an example of a very successful management buyout: The owner got burned out, to use his terminology, when he was in his mid fifties. The general manager, who had become the chief cook and bottle washer by this time anyway, expressed his interest. The owner told him that he would sell to the manager provided the manager could raise sufficient capital. To his surprise, the manager did. The price was less than a third-party sale would generate and the owner had to keep some of the equity and hold some of the debt, but he got enough cash to be free to pursue other interests.

And, as it turned out, the new owner was so enthusiastic that he was able to grow the company very rapidly for about five years. At that time, a large strategic buyer showed up and bought it. Financially, both the new owner and the old one made out well on the deal.

Management buyouts tend to work better with smaller companies. Banks are willing to lend managers money, but not too much. Also, managers will have to put in most of their own net worth. But to reiterate, the best part about management buyouts is that they avoid the hassle of a third-party sale, which we will discuss later.

What to Do with It Part 3: Selling It to the Employees (ESOPs)

An ESOP is an *employee stock ownership plan*. The ESOP societies will tell you that such a plan is the best thing since sliced bread. Since the employees own the company, or at least part of it, they will work hard to make their ownership worth more. Or, at least, that's what's supposed to happen.

More typically, most of the employees don't care about the ESOP very much. They see it as a long-term retirement plan because they cannot get cash out without leaving the company, and even then, they'll receive payments over several years. Of those who do care, many regard the ESOP as about sixth on their list of five concerns about their working conditions and pay. For example, during the 1990s, when United Airlines was an ESOP, its pilots went on slow-down strikes against their employer. However, Southwest Airlines was also a partial ESOP, and its employees were very motivated to help the airline grow. I believe that ESOPs have little or no impact on employee productivity, contrary to the belief of some.

What an ESOP is good for is disposing of some of the
ownership in a company, getting cash, and maintaining
control. The ESOP laws were written to encourage employee
ownership. Accordingly, the percentage of a company that
has been ESOPed is exempt from federal taxes. Because the
company is partially tax-exempt, banks see that it's likely
to be very profitable and are ready and willing to loan the
ESOP money.

How it works, greatly simplified: You create a legal entity
called an ESOP that will own some of the stock. Note that
the employees do not own any stock directly. Then you
have the company appraised by special ESOP appraisers.
You sell to the ESOP some percentage of the company at the
appraised value of the stock. For tax reasons, this must be
at least 30 percent. The bank will set the upper limit based
on their risk assessment. For my company, which had no
debt and was financially very sound, this upper limit was
55 percent when I investigated ESOPs.

After the company sells, say, 55 percent to the ESOP, the
bank loans money to the ESOP and the ESOP pays it to the
owner. Every year the company contributes to the ESOP out
of profits, and the ESOP pays off the loan typically in five
to seven years. This brings out one major disadvantage to
the ESOP: if you want to sell the whole company this way,
you have to do a second ESOP, and the total sale could take
more than a decade.

A second disadvantage is that the total proceeds will usually
be less than for a third-party sale. The ESOP appraiser, you

see, cares only about past numbers, not about potential growth.

A third disadvantage is all the paperwork, including annual appraisals, you have to complete to stay out of trouble and prove you're not cheating the employees.

So what's in it for the employees? Each year they get a certificate telling them the value of the stock they own. Should they terminate employment, the ESOP owes them that much money, although the company can pay it in installments over five years.

What's in it for the owners? They can set up ESOP trustees and keep control even if they own a minority of shares. But, I ask, what good is keeping control if you only own a minority of shares?

The real value of an ESOP is evident when a company has several owners and one wants to get out. Consider a company worth $30 million with three founder-owners. One wants to leave and points out that he should get $10 million in cash. That's fine, but the company has assets, not cash. Solution? Do an ESOP and pay him the $10 million in cash.

The major disadvantage of an ESOP is evident when there is any abrupt change in business conditions and the ESOP participants leave and want to be paid off. I knew an ESOP company that had specialty stores selling office equipment. Over time, the employees built up a business servicing what they sold at customer sites. The servicing of one manufacturer's equipment grew to be about one-third of their total revenues. Suddenly, the manufacturer decided to cut the cord and service the stuff itself. The ESOP company lost one-third of its people overnight, and for the next five years, it had to pay out large cash payments from the ESOP to them. Since its business model had been based on opening new stores whenever it got enough cash to do so, growth stalled. Profits plunged. The stock value, as determined by the appraisers, dived. The remaining employees, seeing their ESOP value decline year after year, were not motivated by ESOP shares, and some were eager to get out instead of letting their stock ride. This company eventually liquidated itself (though the ESOP was not the only reason).

If the company grows rapidly, it can see the opposite effect. Ex-employees will want to cash in their stock instead of letting it ride. Some may even quit in order to cash it in, believing they can get a good payment in each of the next five years.

A large financial institution offered to show my company how it could do an immediate 100 percent ESOP, so my sister and I attended a private meeting at the Union Club in Cleveland, whose membership had included no less than six US presidents, with no less than six persons from different financial institutions. I don't know why they wasted our time.

Their proposal was a 100 percent recapitalization at a price I considered very low. About one-third would be equity provided by the employees' 401(k)s. The stockholders who were selling the company would put up one-third of the equity. This would take the form of unsecured loans and equity that would not start paying off any cash or interest for five years. Most of the rest would be loaned by a bank but secured against assets, and some would be mezzanine debt.[4] If the employees didn't cough up enough from their 401(k)s, the selling stockholders would make up the difference. But, as I later calculated, the debt service (including accumulated interest to the stockholders) would be severe enough that the employees stood a good chance of losing their money. So why would they want to put it up?

Another mistake: assuming finance people are smart enough to do arithmetic.

In summary, I am not a booster of ESOPs. I think they're valuable only in situations where a large minority owner wants out and wants cash, not when a single owner is selling his or her company. Your mileage may vary.

---

4   Mezzanine debt is unsecured debt that, because it is not secured, has high interest payments. As of 2008, 12% to 15% was not uncommon. Also, the lender may insist upon a small portion of the equity and require that the debt not be repaid for several years.

What to Do with It Part 4: Partially Retire and Take Some Cash Off the Table

This plan or a variant is often recommended by someone who hasn't the slightest idea what it means (emotionally, at least) to run a privately held company.

It sounds good. You've accumulated a lot of money either in or outside of the company. If it's inside, it's retained subchapter S earnings (you are sub S, aren't you?). So you pay yourself those earnings. Then you hire or promote someone to be the CEO and, basically, go away.

This is an excellent plan, except it seldom works. For one thing, the semiretired owner is paranoid that the replacement will screw things up. Heck, the replacement actually might screw things up. Then, no matter how serious this really is, the owner will have to return and meddle, not because she might actually need to do so but because doing so is in her DNA. And because the owner has been absent from day-to-day affairs, she really isn't too knowledgeable, and her meddling may make things worse.

So this plan is like selling the company to your kids. Don't do it unless you have your STV in hand, separate from the fortunes of the company, and then don't interfere, if you can. Even then you'll have to dispose of the company later, and later is always when you are older, feebler, and less interested in all the pain associated with selling a company. I really don't recommend this plan.

What to Do with It Part 5: The Third-Party Sale

The title of this book is *Getting Out from Under*. Often the only clean way to do that is the third-party sale.

But, you should not expect it to be easy. It will take a long time and a lot of work. I spent about two thousand hours of my time in the sale process, despite having excellent investment bankers to sell the company. That's one man-year of my time in addition to doing my job.

So go through the process while you're young enough and healthy enough.

To reiterate, start early, and start by calculating your STV (secure threshold value). Then figure out what the company is worth right now. If the value is less than your STV, consider whether you can do something about it in coming years.

Then consider all other options for getting out, and eliminate them if they won't work. Be especially realistic about turning over the business to your children. This should require that they really are competent to run it, as evidenced by their management achievements elsewhere. It also requires that you sell it to them for your STV or more, unless you have the STV otherwise secured. The second-last thing anyone needs is you sitting in a retirement community fretting that your family is destroying the value of your retirement assets, and the last thing anyone needs is for you to show up at the business uninvited and relatively ignorant of recent events to tell everyone what to do. So only turn it over to your kids if you can afford to get out and stay out.

Finally, get some good advice. Network. Find out what others have done, good and bad.

The best advice I can give you is to join Vistage or some similar group (Vistage is the only one with which I have personal experience). This is a group of about twelve thousand CEOs, most of whom own small privately-held companies, who meet monthly in local groups of fifteen or so. Here's why you should belong to Vistage:

1. Your fellow members will include some who are closer to retirement or farther along the sale process than you are. A few may even have already sold their companies. You will also find representatives from all sorts of different companies, including ESOPs.

2. Your Vistage chair, the person who runs the group, plus other chairs in your city can point you to former members and other chairs who have sold businesses.

3. All these people can point you to the investment bankers who are best for selling companies like yours or who are the best ESOP, management buyout, and so on.

4. Vistage meetings give you a whole different outlook on your business problems, and that alone is worth the dues.

Take advantage of any other networking opportunities you have too. I graduated from the Harvard Business School, and one of the most active Harvard Business School clubs is the one in Cleveland, where I lived for a number of years. When I started planning to sell my business, I joined the club and attended their networking functions, where I found members plugged in to merger and acquisition activity. I asked some of these people whom they thought would be a good investment banker for me, and I actually found my eventual investment banker in the club.

Okay, so you didn't go to the Harvard Business School, but you probably did go somewhere. Do the business professors at your old alma mater know somebody? Finally, check out the local chapter of the Association for Corporate Growth (ACG). Dues are nominal; meetings are frequent.

When you find two or three reasonably good investment bankers, check their references. I found that the firm and individual I eventually picked had assisted two people I knew who had sold their businesses.

Oh, and you shouldn't try to sell your business by yourself. Hire an investment banker. Dentists don't do their own dental work, do they? Selling a business, besides the fact that you'll probably only do it once and won't get to practice, is just about as much fun as doing your own root canal.

The Third-Party Sale Process

One problem you'll face right away is telling your team—your key managers—that you're selling the company, but you'll have to tell them because buyers will want to meet them, and you'll need them to make of presentations to buyers to help you sell. They'll probably be a bit scared that you're selling, but you may be surprised. Some of them may think, "At last the skinflint's going away and we'll be able to grow."

If your business is big enough, you'll want to pick five or ten of them to be the selling team. In a manufacturing company, you'd choose the head financial person, the head manufacturing person, the head salesperson, the head engineering person, and maybe a couple of others. Meet with each of them separately to tell them you're selling the company and why. Emphasize that they will probably be better off because the company will go through an orderly transition, something that would not happen if you slumped onto your desk dead with an aneurism. Emphasize too that a buyer will value a good management team and that their positions are probably not in any jeopardy. Explain also that you will probably stay around awhile after the sale to run the company for the new people.

Staying Around?

A short digression: One reason that selling your business is a pain is that the buyer will want you to stay around for a while. Two years is not an atypical period. That means you have to work for somebody else after working for no one for a long time. This would be like the CEO of General Electric being required to work for the new and younger CEO after appointing him or her. You'd better be able to get along with these people.

But what if you don't want to stay around? Well, in general, there are two types of buyers. The first type consists of private equity companies, financial buyers. They may have no management skills that pertain to companies like yours, except for financial management. They will load your company up with debt, expect you to cut costs, expect you to grow where possible, and sell your company in a few years for more than they bought it for. The second type consists of strategic buyers, who want to integrate your products or services into their existing businesses. They have—or think they have—a stable of competent managers in place. They would be more amenable to your leaving and also more willing to fire you.

In either case, you will get a better price, if your company is at all well run, if you tell potential buyers you're eager to stick around and run it. And that can be difficult.

Back to the Sale Process

You don't want key managers to get scared and run off during the sale process. Since I would need my key managers to help me in this effort, I considered what kind of incentives or golden handcuffs to offer them up front. After discussion with my Vistage group, I offered eight people a severance agreement that guaranteed they would get a year's worth of pay if they were terminated within one year of the company's changing control. I also offered the five people who were most important and who would help make management presentations, a stay bonus. This stipulated that they would be paid a bonus of half their annual salary if they stayed six months after any change of control. Our lawyer wrote the first agreement. The second originated from a Vistage group member who had been in a similar situation.

How much should the stay bonus be? You'll get answers all over the map. I selected six months of their pay, as I didn't think anyone would feel slighted because I had a good relationship with each of them, although some of my Vistage group members thought the stay bonus should have been higher. A Vistage colleague who had been through this process told me that her old boss had done the same thing and that she had felt slighted. How do you determine whether this might happen? Mostly by feel. All eight managers had been with me for ten years or more, and I thought they were mostly concerned with their future and the company's, not a short-term bonus. They trusted me to make the right decisions. This particular decision worked out okay.

Once you've determined the stay bonus and the severance, give each manager a document to sign, not just verbal promises. Tell the managers to take the documents home for a couple of days and consult their own lawyers if they want to.

My investment banker assigned a team of three people, two of which we named in the contract, to create a list of possible buyers, both strategic and financial, and I added some names of strategic buyers. To the listed prospects, the investment banker sent out a teaser, a short document outlining the company and asking the recipients asked to express their interest, note approximately how much they thought the company would be worth, and note how they intended to finance the acquisition.

When the prospects returned this, the banker mailed them an offering memorandum, a booklet we had prepared about our company. This is commonly called "the book" in the industry. The book is a summary of your company—what it does, five years of financial history, who your competitors are, why you win, who your personnel are, who your customers are, and your plans for future years. You and your people will have to spend a lot of time helping the investment banker write this.

Figuring out whom to solicit can be either easy or hard. For instance, a friend owned a paper distributorship. There were several large distributorships engaged in roll-ups, buying smaller distributors and tying all of them together. These were obvious buyers.

My company had no obvious buyers. It had three product lines that each used some similar technologies and manufacturing facilities, but each was sold to a different industrial market. Buyers have a hard time coping with that. In particular, strategic buyers want to buy a company that synergizes with their existing operations, and strategic buyers for my company each related to only one of the three product lines.

Financial buyers had a hard time understanding what technical products did, and it can be aggravating that they couldn't see the benefits of technological innovation for a company. That said, it was interesting to me that the financial buyers I met seemed to be smarter than the strategic buyers. I think this is because in companies which are strategic buyers, the smartest people were involved with making and selling their products, not mergers and acquisitions, whereas at private equity companies, their main business is M&A, so that's where the smart people were. They were smart but not necessarily perceptive.

Data Rooms in the Twenty-First Century

Serious buyers will be invited to root through a plethora of your data. In times past, this was contained in a special room, perhaps at your attorney's office. Nowadays it is all digitized and on a special website with a password. This is much more convenient for you and the buyers and allows you to find out who looked at what and for how long.

Management Presentations

The next step is to invite the serious firms, six in my case, to a management presentation. This was the first time I met any of the prospects. For each of these, we met at a hotel meeting room early in the morning for a PowerPoint presentation that, including breaks, lasted until about 2:00

in the afternoon. Then we took the prospects on a plant tour. Finally, in most cases, we had dinner. Each attendee got a thick book containing reproductions of the PowerPoint slides.

From my company, my VP of manufacturing, my three VPs in charge of sales and engineering for each of the three business units, the controller, my sister, and I attended these presentations. This means that all these people were tied up for sometimes twelve hours at a time. Further, from seeing all these managers disappear for hours followed by tours of the plant for a bunch of strange people, all the employees surmised that the company was going to be sold. My cover story was that we were considering recapitalization, something most employees didn't know the meaning of, in order to have more funds for future growth. They accepted this largely because (a) we had been growing a lot in recent years, and (b) the culture in our company was one that trusted management. Nevertheless, the cat was probably out of the bag.

All six prospects were private equity (financial) buyers, not strategic buyers. They attended with anywhere from two to nine people each, some of whom were pretty smart but most of whom struck me as stupid, arrogant, and clueless, for they failed to understand what we did and failed to ask any questions about the five or six things that I thought might be the most important. Some of them brought along manufacturing "experts" whose experience seemed narrow and irrelevant to me.

The actions of even serious buyers will vary all over the map, but I think the following events are more or less typical. We set a deadline for offers, and the following occurred:

The first firm attended the presentation with two people, did not stay for dinner, and made a written offer with no further discussion. It was evident their lawyer had spent a lot of time commenting on our draft purchase agreement. I rejected the offer because it was too low.

At this point, I will interject and remind you that you need to get your lawyer and accountant involved before the sale process even starts. By this point, my accountant had already estimated how much he thought the company would sell for, including estimated taxes, and the investment banker had independently estimated it. In other words, "too low" means too low relative to what these experts said, not relative to my emotions.

The second firm made an offer at the same price but with interesting financing: they would put up 25 percent of the price as equity, we stockholders would put up 12.5 percent, and loan the buyer 12.5 percent, unsecured and at low interest, and then the buyer would borrow 50 percent from a large regional bank. These guys asked for a private meeting with my sister and me to present this as a hypothetical offer. We rejected them. I could borrow that much money from the bank without them.

The third bunch seemed to resent the fact that we were successful and profitable. They did not make an offer. They wanted instead to find companies with problems that were easy for them to correct, so they could increase the value with little effort. We were not low-hanging fruit.

The representatives of the fourth prospective buyer simply acted like jerks. We had little chemistry. They made no offer.

The fifth one spent two weeks asking dumb questions, and each question necessitated our doing several hours of work. It soon appeared to me they were getting ready to make on offer for only one of our three product lines. We told them to either make an offer for the whole company or go away. They made a low offer for the company and went away.

The sixth group represented a first-class private equity firm with an excellent reputation. Their chief investigator thought we were a really prize acquisition but couldn't convince their president, who was perturbed because he had figured out we were really in three separate businesses (a fact that was evident from the front page of our website, by the way). How could his firm, which owned only about thirty other companies, keep track of all these disparate businesses? The firm did verbally mention a price that was higher than the other offers, but we told them not to waste their money on the postage stamp for the paperwork because it also was low.

So, after all that work, six strikes and we were out. From what I can tell, this is not atypical.

Postmortem

One problem was that we were rapidly growing. As late as November in the year we signed the contract with the investment banker, we were not certain whether sales would surpass our all-time record. As it turned out, they did so with room to spare. EBITDA for that year set another all-time record. We also had an all-time record backlog at the end of the year and were telling the buyers we would do a 27 percent increase in sales and increase EBITDA by 50 percent in the following year,[5] based on this backlog and some other fundamentals I will not dwell upon here. The buyers simply would not believe this. They based their offers on past results as if our growth was flat, and some of them even wondered if the prior twelve months had been an unusual spike.

For some reason, trailing twelve-month earnings (TTM EBITDA) seems to be a be-all and end-all in the private equity industry when determining offering value.

So the obvious strategy was to stop selling the company and wait for actual results to reflect the shipping of our large backlog. A second obvious strategy was for me to go out and find some buyers myself, rather than have only the investment banker do this. That's what happens when owners are obsessive-compulsive. When we did find buyers again, we would qualify them more thoroughly before wasting a lot of time on management presentations.

---

5   At the end of the second quarter of that year, it became pretty clear that these sales and EBITDA forecasts would be exceeded, by the way.

How could I find buyers? Simple. Various brokers had called me up for years, so I let them know what the facts were and, in a one-hour telephone conversation with their principals, gave them some brief financial facts, some projections, and told them what digit the price would have to start with as a minimum. I turned them over to the investment bankers if they passed my test and told them to go away if they couldn't stomach the technical nature of our three businesses.

The full process then went like this:

1. I had my telephone conversation (followed by the confidentiality agreement, offering memorandum, etc.).

2. The potential buyer came to Cleveland with one or two people and had a two-hour lunch with me and one person from my investment banking firm. None of my other people attended. I gave the buyer a plant tour.

3. The survivors got a management presentation.

4. The investment bankers got in early and constant contact with the buyers and emphasized that they should go away if they were going to make a low-ball offer.

Second Time at Bat

This process yielded a better class of buyer. Four serious offers emerged, from a group of about twelve at the first step and perhaps eight firms after the second—six private equity firms who seemed more on the ball than the first group and two strategic buyers.

Here is a summary of the results:

One private equity firm had a partner who was a neighbor and a friend of one of the members of my Vistage group, and that's how we got together. After we had met for lunch with this person and taken him and one other on a plant trip, his people made a written offer for a reasonable price, although it contained an earn-out for subsequent years. This offer was also vague about how the deal would be financed—it said financing was TBD (alarm bells went off).

Now, I am very skeptical about earn-outs, which are processes in which some of the price will be held back and only paid if earnings in future years exceed a certain target. If you're gone after the sale, you have no control over this at all, and if you're still running the place after the sale, you only have partial control. When you're working for the new owners, what if you think that x is the right thing to do to increase earnings but they think that y is? What if resentments force them to terminate you and your replacement is a goofball who hurts earnings?

A worse problem was that representatives of this firm didn't meet with any of my managers, despite our offer to set this up.[6] They said they could do this during the due-diligence period after we agreed to negotiate exclusively with them (more alarm bells went off). My investment banker

---

6   By this time, I had noticed that the more exposure a firm had to my managers, the greater its enthusiasm became.

suggested to the firm's president that we could come to their office and give them a briefing. The president thought this was a good idea and said he would get back to us. He never did. On occasion, my contact at this firm claimed my investment bankers were discriminating against his firm because they didn't answer questions by some deadline he wanted to set, although in reality, we had told the president why we couldn't answer that quickly, and he had accepted this but not told my contact. All very strange, and definite reasons to run away. If you can't get along with a buyer at this stage, how would you get along after the sale?

I found the next firm, a family-owned private equity firm, through a broker. They made two more trips to Cleveland to interview my managers and ask questions after their presentation, and they spent a lot of time in the digital data room. They made sure we met all five of their senior partners. When I told them one of my key people might retire soon, they asked for one-on-one interviews with the three people who might take over his duties. They were thorough, smart, and seemed to have integrity. They made a good offer and named the banks they would use to finance the deal.

Their offer required the stockholders to buy some of the equity and also to hold a note, lending them money. They also stated they would set aside 10 percent of the equity for stock options for our managers. This was the first offer that I could have felt comfortable accepting.

How the Second Bite of the Apple Works

At this point I digress to explain, for those who may not be familiar with it, how a second payoff can occur. It works in general with private equity firms but not with strategic buyers. Strategic buyers intend to keep your business forever. A private equity firm, by contrast, intends to sell it in about five years. PE firms raise commitments from university endowment funds, retirement plans, and other institutions with long time horizons and then establish a fund. The fund, which typically has a life of ten years, buys a bunch of companies. Later the fund sells them, distributes the money, and disappears. The private equity company raises a new fund.

I will use hypothetical numbers, but the ratios are real. Suppose you sell a company for $50 million to a private equity firm. They are going to try to borrow $35 million, so the equity is $15 million. Suppose they ask you to buy back $3 million in equity as part of the deal. Here is what happens:

1. You get paid $47 million (Ahem, that's pretax. Get your CPA to compute the taxes on that).

2. You own 20 percent of the equity even though you only put up 6 percent of the sale price. Most of the sale price was debt.

3. If they pay off the debt and sell the company in five years for $50 million, you get a $10-million return on your $3-million investment!

4. If they sell the company for $100 million, your $3 million has grown to $20 million!

5. If the business goes into Chapter 7, guess what? You still get to keep the $47 million (less taxes).

Yes, it's legal, and yes, Virginia, there is a Santa Claus. And your money is subject to capital gains treatment as this is written, but you'll pay lower taxes than income tax rates.

Q: How long do you have to keep the stock?

A: Usually until the other firm sells the company again, about five years on average.

Second Time at Bat (Continued)

The last prospective buyer, a well-known local private equity company, won. Here's why:

1. Their offer was 6 percent higher than the other firm's offer.

2. Their offer was more thorough. For instance, they included letters of intent from their financial sources. Nothing is worse than an offer contingent on financing falling through because the buyer can't get the financing.

3. They spent more time meeting with us after the presentation, more time in the digital data room, and so on. They asked intelligent questions, and

they had people with industrial experience, not just mere bean counters. Good chemistry.

4. Points 2 and 3 meant there was less chance of the deal falling apart during due diligence.

5. The stockholders didn't have to loan them any money. The firm's reinvestment of equity deal was also better because the representatives had sold their bankers on the deal, even having them attend the management presentation.

6. They set aside 15 percent of equity for stock options for management, not just 10 percent.

7. They were local, so I could check up on them with various contacts.

8. I checked all the references they provided, talking with each one for about forty-five minutes each.

9. My managers liked them the best.

10. They had a good reputation.

So why hadn't my investment bankers approached this firm in the first go-round? The answer is they did but were told the firm was interested only in buying companies above a certain revenue threshold, and when we started the process, we were under that. When we selected this company as the buyer and signed the letter of intent, we were way over that. In fact, sales were 40 percent over that for the year after the sale.

I guess this was another case of financial people looking backward, not projecting forward.

What about Strategic Buyers?

There were two. The first was a division of a large conglomerate that buys about thirty companies per year. One of our sales engineers suspected we were for sale and blabbed to one of their sales guys at a trade show, so they called up. They were really interested in our oldest product line but also intrigued by a second product line, saying they had always wanted to enter that business and opining that their international sales force could sell the products overseas better.[7] They were confused by our third product line.

These guys lasted through step 2 of the vetting process. At that time they said they didn't want the part of the business that originally piqued their interest and wanted to buy the third part instead of the second. Since we were not a department store, we insisted they had to buy all the stuff or nothing. They evaporated.

The second strategic was a very large Fortune 500 company in a somewhat stodgy industry. They were actively acquiring companies with a view toward becoming less stodgy by making acquisitions in growth industries, and they had made several. They were also one of our customers. They approached us quite by accident during

---

7   I have found that many large companies think they can beat smaller companies at selling, though most of them can't.

our process, although they got in on things the same week as the eventual winner.

Their problem was that it took them a long time to do anything. It took them two weeks to sign the confidentiality agreement. Then, after receiving the offering memorandum, they complained a week later that it had not arrived, and then they found it in their e-mail. They rescheduled and delayed the management presentation a couple of times. Despite all this, I thought they were a first-class outfit, and they asked serious questions.

Each serious buyer had been asked to submit a letter of intent (LOI), with a firm price and terms by a certain date. Instead, this strategic firm named a price range instead, from $0.75x$ to x, where x was the approximate price the two most serious contenders, private equity firms both, had offered. Why such a wide range? They said their CFO was unwilling to pay more for our last year's results (once again, backward-looking financial people). We said we were not selling our old results, pointing out our recent rapid growth. They later raised their range to $0.875x$ to x, but told us that they didn't think they could quite get to x.

Another problem for us was that they required an exclusive negotiating period to narrow their range, and this would take six weeks (later reduced to three weeks). We told them flat out that others were offering a firm number and that we could not give them an exclusive because it could lose us the other, higher bidders. So we stalled them off for two weeks while we negotiated the LOI with the best prospective buyer.

When our investment banker told this strategic that we had signed the agreement with the eventual successful buyer, they got irate and called me to complain about how they had been treated. They said they were prepared to offer *x* plus $4 million.

Q: Why didn't you? We told you about what the other guys were bidding.

A: We would have if you had told us you needed that much. I'm pretty sure I could have sold it to my bosses. (Honest! That's what the representative said.)

They also complained they didn't have enough time. When they heard that I liked the stock options two of the buyers offered for my people and me, they countered with their matching 401(k) program, which was not as good as the one my company already had.

I think this company believed its own propaganda. Its representatives implied several times that they were a "solid, honest Midwest manufacturing company" (read: they were the Virgin Mary) and financial buyers were crooked shysters (read: a bunch of whores). In fact, they once told us we should be willing to accept less from a strategic buyer like them than from a private equity firm and went so far as to send me reprints of *Wall Street Journal* articles about financial shenanigans in the private equity industry.

And after I told them we had already signed the LOI with its exclusivity period with the private equity firm, they called the head honcho at our investment bank and complained about the lack of professionalism of the people handling the deal, an opinion I did not share.

Which brings up the eleventh reason for selecting the ultimate winning buyer: I had to work for these people for a while!

I believe that if the deal had fallen through during due diligence, we would still have been able to revisit negotiations with this buyer, and conclude a sale successfully.

At last, we signed an agreement with a buyer. That process had taken ten whole months, which is not atypical, and the process was not over. What did the agreement say? Merely that they agreed to buy our company at a certain price under certain terms. There was a sixty-day exclusivity period during which we could not negotiate with any other buyer. During that time, the buyers had a right to pore over our data and ask anything or see anything they wanted, a process known as "due diligence." At the end of that time, they would proceed with paying us, and owning us, unless they found something they didn't like. Due diligence has lots of outs, but the buyer is unlikely to exercise any for frivolous reasons because of the time and money that the buyer has to invest to find any.

The Joys of Due Diligence!

Due diligence is a very trying time. A lot of deals fall apart during this time. The buyer typically sends a lot of people into your company to pry everywhere and take up the time of your people, particularly your financial people. If they find anything they don't like or that's a surprise, they can use that as an excuse to walk away.

When Reliance Electric Company, a billion-dollar firm that was both a competitor, vendor, and customer of ours, announced to all their employees and the press that they had agreed to be acquired by Siemens AG, a herd of bean counters and lawyers descended on Reliance. At length, the Siemens people told Reliance that they (Reliance) were valuing their field-repair depots too highly and that their pension obligations, even though they had stopped offering new employees defined-benefit pensions many years earlier, were actually higher than Reliance had said they were. Siemens wanted a discount for this stuff. Reliance said no. The deal fell apart, and all parties had egg on their faces.

With the prospect of all these people prying around my company, I wanted to tell the employees that we had tentatively agreed to sell since I believe in telling the truth instead of letting rumors fly. But the buyer did not want us to do this until the actual close, which turned out to be three months off, not two as the LOI had specified.

Due diligence imposed a tremendous burden on our management for those three months. The first phase involved several different consulting firms hired by the buyer:

1. A CPA firm audited our books, our accounting system, and the CPAs who had prepared our annual audits. The burden here was that they asked a lot of questions, and each answer generated more questions.

2. An environmental consulting firm from Atlanta visited us for a week. Their total time with us exceeded the time I had spent in the two years prior to get three Phase II environmental surveys completed.

3. A law firm required us to gather together all corporate documents, permits, and other papers and also a large quantity of our contracts with customers. This was more difficult than it might seem. For instance, we found that we had never obtained an occupancy or boiler permit for our largest facility.

4. An operations consultant spent an entire week in our manufacturing areas, not only checking us out

but also coming up with ideas for improvement after the closing.

5. An HR consultant interviewed my key managers and me in detail. The buyer's key people also held individual meetings with all my managers.

6. Three IT consultants spent several days checking our MIS system.

7. A marketing research firm met with us and then requested names and phone numbers of two hundred customers from each of our three business units. They then called them, under the guise of doing marketing research, and produced a profile of our products' acceptance and opportunities for growth. To my amazement, they did a good job at this. The three people doing the calling were no telemarketing dummies. Their resumes included stints at McKinsey, Boston Consulting Group, and Booz Allen Hamilton.

8. This was a tremendous amount of intrusion, and it coincided with our company's growing about 35 percent per annum.

So how did we keep this secret? The cover story was still that we were considering taking in some outside investors to help us grow and that their lenders wanted to make sure we were telling them the right stories. By the end of the process, however, I became convinced that every employee knew we were being sold. I think morale remained high only because the employees in general had confidence that

I would do the right thing. The top managers, of course, had been told they would be allowed to purchase some of the stock and also would get stock options, though the amounts hadn't been specified yet.

Other Due Diligence Tasks

While all this was going on, we had to give two presentations to the buyer's proposed banks and other lenders. This involved presentations about as elaborate as our initial presentations to proposed buyers, which means that all things considered, our managers and I gave twelve full-blown, multi-hour presentations and a plant tour to various people. These lender presentations included people from Cleveland, Chicago, New York, and Minneapolis.

Another task was to compute the required working capital—the current assets needed to run the business after closing. If this amount of capital weren't available on the day of the close, as determined later by an audit, the price would go down. Similarly, if more were available, the price would go up. The investment bankers, who had a really good financial guy, negotiated the required working capital, and our CPA firm reviewed it. Before this experience, I had thought that the investment bank's basic contribution would be selling, but, in fact, they accomplished many other, chiefly financial, things.

I think it was an advantage that my company, the buyer, the investment banking firm, our law firm, and the buyer's law firm were all local and had known each other at least by reputation before this. You can control this insofar as your investment banker and law firm are concerned, and it was lucky for us that the buyer was also local.

Trouble: How the Deal almost Fell Apart

As I said, a lot of acquisitions break up during the due diligence period. Our crisis occurred about six weeks into the process, in September.

The buyer had determined that our financial management was our weakest card compared with our technical excellence, sales and marketing, production, and quality control. Incidentally, I agreed and had discussed this freely with the buyer. My philosophy was to hide absolutely nothing from them during due diligence. We had also discussed the need to hire a CFO for our company after the closing, as we really didn't have one and didn't think our controller could advance to the position. Perhaps for this reason, the buyer spent a lot of time on our numbers.

At any rate, they discovered a $400,000 error in our reported YTD earnings (which weren't audited until the end of the year). This resulted from a systematic error in our MIS system, which we knew about, and the accrual of which our accountant corrected for by adjusting a fudge factor each month before the end-of-the-year audit. However, because of the company's growth and the accountant's workload, the error had become larger, and he had neglected to adjust it. I knew none of this before the buyer discovered it.

Buyers don't like surprises during due diligence.

In August, coincidentally, we had a bad sales month, and our receivables over ninety days reached a new high.

All these things taken together set off alarm bells. The buyer had apparently based everything on an assumption that EBITDA that year, which had three months to run, would be a certain amount, which, of course, I had forecast. Coincidentally. I had done this, my first ever EBITDA forecast, months earlier. Now the buyer doubted that much EBITDA could be achieved.

We switched gears and spent a lot of hours tracking receivables and issuing a report on each and every one of them. We solved that problem.

Next, we took each project of the hundreds in-house and analyzed scheduled ship dates in October, November, December; the likelihood that they would slip to another month; printed out the costs charged to each of them to date; estimated the percentage complete and the costs to go; and thus forecasted EBITDA for the remaining three months of the year. I forecasted numbers that seemed quite high, but as a reality check, noted that TTM EBITDA had been even higher. Several lengthy reports and two long meetings with the buyers followed, and they accepted our conclusions about this.

However, that left the $400,000 accounting error, and possibly others. We bored into our numbers with a tremendous amount of scrutiny. Our controller froze into immobility like a deer in the headlights. The problem was only solved after the investment bankers spent many hours working through the problems with him and with MIS generating reports. These showed that our reserves every year going back *five* years had been sufficient to cover such adjustments, and it seemed likely this pattern would hold in the near future. This satisfied everyone.

However, in the process, the buyer discovered another anomaly of our system. When we constructed something for inventory, such as a product or subassembly, we put labor, material, and overhead into it. When we took the product or subassembly out, it came out as material only. The buyer wanted us to reconcile $3 million of "missing" stuff. After a hundred hours or so, we did this—sort of.

Finally, I realized that we had no system of accurately estimating project costs until after shipment. We estimated the cost, priced it, and then learned later if we met the estimate. One thousand hours of engineering may have been budgeted, and one thousand hours may have been expended, but our only means of telling if those thousand hours had actually been usefully spent was by anecdotally asking the engineers or by noticing that the project had been on the floor too long. I resolved to fix this after the acquisition. In fact, it suddenly dawned on me that our entire financial system told us where we had been, not where we are going. It was like driving a car by looking in the rearview mirror.

The trouble with accountants in general was that most of them thought their job was to reflect the past and pay the taxes correctly. Well, that was fine, but I thought their job was to predict the future too. If I'm driving a car along the highway, I want to know how fast I'm going right now, how close I'm driving to the side of the road, and how far I've got to go. Accountants are more interested in how far I've driven and how long it has taken. That was useful, but not too useful for running a company in real time.

About five years before I sold the company, I established financial goals for each of my three product lines. The guy running the largest one compared his year-to-date performance with the objectives each month. In November, though, the accountants reallocated $900,000 of costs to his operations, greatly reducing his results. He—and his managers—were perturbed by this, and they should have been, but the accountants couldn't understand why. After all, they said, the $900,000 would have been subtracted during the annual audit in April of the following year.

The solution to this kind of thinking is to get new accountants, or reeducate the old ones.

Arguments Between the Stockholders

The buyer's letter of intent mentioned that $3 million of equity would be set aside for *management* to purchase immediately. Our lawyer and my sister thought that this meant that my sister and I would each buy $1.5 million, when actually, the buyer meant that I should buy $2.5 million and four managers collectively could buy $500,000. Why should my sister buy any? The buyer's intent, after all, was to incentivize the people who would manage the company going forward. After some discussion with me, they reneged a little and fixated on $2.0 million for me, $0.5 million for my sister, and $0.5 million for the managers.

Now, I thought this would be fine because the buyer would *obviously* welcome additional equity, so my sister could buy as much as she wanted to take the management portion above $3 million. I thought $3 million was a minimum. Wrong!

In fact, the buyer did not want more equity because that would dilute their payoff when the company was sold again in five years.

My sidebar discussions with my sister got nowhere. I resented the fact that I had made all the rain, at least from my point of view, and she was going to benefit so much. While I felt that I had a strong case under the stockholders' agreement we had in place, I didn't want a bitter fight. The amount in contention, I calculated, would not be a huge portion of my net worth in five years, depending on what the buyer resold the company for at that time, so I told them that my sister and I would each get the opportunity to purchase $1.25 million of stock and that was the way it was going to be. After a little arguing, they bought that.

But all things considered, we had fewer family business problems than many other companies.

More Due Diligence Jollies

As if due diligence didn't cause any unnecessary angst, here are some other items that would not warrant a thought if we weren't selling the company:

The Change of Structure Problem

The buyer decided that in a few years, when they flipped it, the company would possibly be more valuable if each of the three businesses were, in fact, separate corporations. This created tax advantages, but only if the split were done before the acquisition. So, a new contract obligated the buyer to pay all the extra accounting and legal costs if the acquisition wasn't made, and one day before the close, a lawyer went to the Ohio Statehouse to file the appropriate whatevers. For these contracts, I was required to sign my name 450 times on various papers that I did not, and have not, read. A lawyer sat across from me and handed me each page to sign in turn.

And so we became a holding company owning three operating companies the day before closing.

The Big Contract Novation Problem

We had contracts with a lot of companies and with the US government that had to be *novated*, or assigned to the new owners. Prior to the close, the buyer wanted us to obtain, in writing, assertions from our customers that they would novate the contracts.

Have you ever tried to get a government employee to do something outside the normal chain of procedures? We eventually forgot about this.

The $8.8 Million Contract Deal

During due diligence, we got a huge contract from a near-bankrupt company that was reselling goods to the Air Force, which had awarded this contract seven years earlier to a third company that defaulted after spending a lot of Air Force money. It took the Air Force seven years to get its act together and reprocure these items, and this time it only allowed two companies—each of which had built this stuff in the past—to submit bids. Unfortunately, one of these was bankrupt and the other nearly so.

The nearly-bankrupt company teamed with us and submitted an $8.8-million bid. They stated right in their proposal that my company would build the stuff and pay their company a $1-million royalty. Further, the bid stated, each payment upon shipment of a unit would go to us, not the bidder, and we would then pay the bidder. This was all up front, satisfied the Air Force's terms, and wasted $1 million of the taxpayers' money.

The only fly in the ointment is that our "partner" wanted the $1 million in advance. We preferred to pay a small portion upon each unit's shipment, to ensure their continued cooperation. We eventually agreed to pay $350,000 in advance and the rest in increments upon shipment of each unit.

At that time, I reasoned that we were about to spend $350,000 but that the company, which was supposed to be bought by then, wouldn't get any benefit until after the sale. So I explained all this to the buyer and got them to raise the sale price by $350,000. As it turned out, they got a bargain. The contract was more profitable than we had estimated.

Massive Growth during the Negotiations

Due diligence was supposed to take sixty days, according to the contract, but it actually took a bit over ninety. During all this time, we had continued to grow. But I decided this would be a very bad time to attempt to renegotiate price, except for cases like the $350,000 cost noted above. For one thing, it was late 2007 and fairly obvious that the whole US economy in general and bank lending in particular were declining. For another, we had just come through the big accounting error and the low August results.

Switching from Due Diligence to Closing

One thing that did happen, though, was much more scrutiny of our financial history toward the end. I listened in on a phone call in which a junior employee from the buyer asked our controller about some $9,000 expense from five years in the past. I eventually told the investment banker to tell the buyer that the due diligence exclusivity period had expired and that we would answer no more questions except for procedural questions leading to closing the deal. I don't know what or how he told the buyer, but the deal closed shortly after that.

Incidentally, all such deals are debt-free and cash-free, which means the buyer will subtract debt from the purchase price, but you get to keep the cash. On the day of closing, make sure you collect the petty cash as well. In our case, it amounted to about $2,000 in small bills and change.

You've Sold the Business: Now What?

The sale is complete. A lot of money has been wired to your checking account. Despite that, you feel some remorse.

Depending on what terms you've worked out, you're either unemployed but rich or employed by the new owners and rich. Either way, you've almost certainly got a non-compete contract with the new owners for a period of several years. If you've sold to a private equity company, you probably also have a stock option deal of some sort that promises to pay you some extra money later, when the new owners sell the company. A couple of months after the close, there will be an audit of working capital, and one party may have to fork over some cash to the other. And finally there's an escrow account with generally 10 to 15 percent held back for twelve to eighteen months in case the buyer discovers there was any misrepresentation, deliberate or accidental, during the sale process.

Even if you're not the CEO, you will still probably be on the payroll as a consultant for a while and may also be on the board. Since all sorts of permutations can happen, let's assume you're the CEO. Your lawyer has worked out an employment contract that says the company must pay you a certain salary and bonus for a year or two. If they want to get rid of you, they have to pay you to stay home, but if you want to quit, they can stop paying you. However, it may also say that your rights to additional stock when they sell the company vest over, say, a five year period, which means you can't just walk out without forfeiting some of the second bite of the apple.

Your contract may even include an earn-out provision, though, as noted, I believe you should do everything possible to avoid earn-outs, including walking away from the deal if you need to.

So what's it like working for the new guys, especially since you haven't worked for anyone but yourself for years?

First, the new owners will require much greater detail than you've been used to providing in financial reporting, meaning you will likely end up adding people to your financial department who will create a lot more reports. Second, there will be a more detailed budgeting process than before. Things you previously considered noise-level variations will have to be explained in detail. You will be asked to get your team together and come up with x of proposed cost savings and then document whether you made it.

The new owners will meet with you, either in person or over the phone, once a week.

In some cases, the new owners may fixate on a member of your team, suggesting that you fire him or her for reasons you don't think are reasonable. They will suggest that you visit other portfolio companies they own and incorporate those companies' best practices, even if they wouldn't apply to your company. In one case I know of, the owner took to calling the CEO at home on Sunday nights to rant and rave and swear at him.

My owners were more reasonable, although I did have to spend time fighting them off. They suggested that my manufacturing VP visit a certain other company to look at their lean manufacturing techniques. After the visit, they complained that my VP didn't have enough initiative to follow up with that CEO to learn more. I explained that that CEO had other things to do besides help us pro bono. He had just laid off 40 percent of his employees, including himself, while we had beaten our EBITDA target. Perhaps, I intimated, the other company should have concentrated more on sales and less on lean manufacturing.

Then our VP offered to show the owners some cost-reduction rearrangements he had done in the assembly area. They complained to me about these too, saying that we should have eliminated our machine shop and subcontracted out all the machining. I explained that we *had* subcontracted all our long runs but needed the machine shop because contract machine shops didn't do very short and quick runs. For instance, a customer would call us up with an emergency. We would charge them about 300 percent of the normal price but get them the item in a couple of days. They appreciated that, and it more than paid for the machine shop.

But next the owners claimed that we should shut down the machine shop because it took up half of a certain building and we would need the space for more assembly. I measured the space, which was much less than half the building, and also calculated how much assembly space we could conceivably need, demonstrating that we should—and were going to—keep the machine shop.

We kept it, but the owners, for some reason, deepened their animosity toward the VP.

The new owners hired two outside board members and got some other members from the PE company. The outside guys, while smart, didn't know very much about businesses like ours. One complained that we didn't adequately explain what was going on. Predictably, this resulted in more and more PowerPoint slides being added at each board meeting. Then we got complaints that the board meetings were too long.

The new owners weren't totally unreasonable, though. Our fabrication shop was running at maximum capacity due to our growth, and one machine, a computerized punch press, was both the workhorse and the bottleneck. We found a used punch press in very good condition, and I wanted to buy it for several hundred thousand dollars. This was important because the new ones used slightly different software, but this used one, which had been very hard to find, would eliminate a lot of software costs. The owners did let me buy it, after a lot of tooth gnashing, even though it wasn't in the budget.

Immediately upon taking control, the new owners asked me to give most of my direct reports a raise and to put them on an incentive bonus plan. After iterating this a few times, the incentive bonus plan amounted to a big financial objective for each person plus two small nonfinancial objectives. If all three were met, the manager could get 30 percent of base pay as a bonus. If they were exceeded, the bonus would be more than 30 percent. The first year this was offered, the bonuses exceeded 40 percent, mostly due to increasing sales because of our new product introduction (R&D).

One very bright spot: We had been working on a high-torque-at-zero-speed motor control for a few years. Now it had progressed to the point where we wanted to do an experiment at a prospective customer's site. This experiment would cost around $500,000. If successful, it would lead to more product development and eventually some revenue, though we couldn't be certain of the timing or amount. So I suggested to the owners that we approve this non-budgeted expense. Intrigued, they agreed, though not before we put in a lot of extra work explaining it.

Nevertheless, explaining everything to these people became tedious. I can't really blame them because, having spent a lot of their money, they had a right to see where it was going. But here is one example. They were concerned that our aerospace division had too much work-in-process inventory. They naturally blamed this on the aforementioned VP of manufacturing and almost demanded I fire him. I explained that in the custom test equipment business[8] the reason the stuff was late getting shipped was because of customer changes (for which we were mostly paid), late engineering (which was necessary before ordering parts, and not under the VP's control), and a big rush of orders that caused a bottleneck. In short, it had nothing to do with manufacturing. I told them this, but I'm not sure they ever believed it.

So, after two years of working for the private equity firm, I was getting a little tired of it. Just about then my employment contract was up. The two head honchos of the PE company asked to have dinner with me, and we all agreed to hire my replacement.

The hiring process took nine months. It is surprising to some to realize that, however much PE firms know about M&A, they really don't know much about normal business tasks, including hiring people. First, it took several months to hire the right headhunter, one acceptable to my bosses. Then the right headhunter presented a list of candidates I didn't think were very good, but we invited three of them to our city for the usual treatment, and it turned out that two of them were very good. The PE guys didn't like those two. Instead they liked an individual who had worked for a division of GE with 6,000 unionized blue collar workers and about 65 white-collar employees and whose major claim to fame was laying off many of the blue-collar workers. In contrast, our own culture was supportive and union-free, and we had about 200 salaried people out of 450

---

8   What we actually made was custom test equipment for aircraft applications, not aerospace equipment, though they insisted on benchmarking us against the second industry.

employees, including 100 engineers. I could have imagined a more appropriate background. But the head PE guy insisted we hire someone from an "academy company," in which class he put GE. I had little respect for GE managers because much of our growth over the years had come from stripping their peripheral business away, but by this time, I just wanted the pain to stop.

This GE guy came back for a second visit. I met him for breakfast, he met our managers, and then I was the last one to meet with him before he left to go to dinner with two PE guys. During this second meeting I learned for the first time that he expected $750,000 per year in base salary, which was way out of our range. I asked him if he didn't think the job would be a bit of a comedown. He replied, "Well, X and Y [the two PE guys] will just have to make it worth my while." As he was driving downtown to meet them, I called X and Y and told them this. X said, "Well, he needs to realize his big payoff will come when the next PE company—the one we sell to—buys the company. He'll get a good incentive then." Somehow I didn't think he would believe this.

I also didn't think our headhunter was competent. As it turned out, we ended up with only one candidate who met the academy-company hurdle, even though he had lost two recent jobs. Further, he had been referred to the headhunter by X from the PE company.

Some headhunter!

So this candidate was offered the job, but the PE guys first asked me to read the offer letter. I told them it wasn't a good recruiting letter, and I suggested we plagiarize the letter I'd written two years before when I'd hired a CFO. I sent them a copy, and they did that.

The guy they hired was pretty bad in my opinion. All he knew how to do was make squiggly charts, most of which didn't mean much. He came up with the idea of firing fifty people to impress the PE people that we were saving money, he said. As near as I could tell, the people were selected almost at random. He asked what I thought of this plan and received an honest answer! Morale and earnings later plummeted.

One of the people the guy fired was my son, a salesman who was closing a $6.15 million order right then. The new CEO apparently felt awkward having anybody from the previous regime around. I explained that this would jeopardize the order, but he wouldn't listen. At this point, he and I had a serious disagreement, but my son stayed only until he had closed the order.

Later this worthy decided to fire all the maintenance and janitorial staff, and the next day he contracted with an outside firm for these services and got the firm to hire the same people we had employed. The maintenance people, who went around the plants all day talking to people while emptying wastebaskets, were very unhappy. The cost to the company went up. So why do this? "To lower fixed costs," he said!

I received an Email from our agents in India who thought I was still CEO (I still had my company Email address) complaining that our sales efforts were incompetent and our competitor was going to get a big order. I sent this to our new CEO. As far as I could tell, he did nothing with it and didn't inform sales. The competitor got a very large order.

At that time, I had an office and a desk at one of the company's divisions for a year and was carrying out my consulting contract. Employees would come to me and ask me to tell the CEO about problems. I asked them why they didn't do that themselves, and they said they were afraid to talk to him. I stopped using that office.

During the entire term of the consulting contract, I was never officially asked one question by my replacement except for my opinion on firing fifty people. I believe this cost the company several millions in sales. The CEO treated any suggestion as criticism, and the head of the PE group had told me not to complain about anything or criticize, so I didn't. I went to the board meetings, smiled, collected my board pay, and waited for my stock options, which eventually paid me more money than I had anticipated, to fully vest.

About a year later, this CEO wangled himself a position with the first of our three companies the PE firm later sold. After he started spending time there, the VP of the division called him a fruitcake and quit, the international sales manager quit, the highest paid salesperson quit, and the sales manager quit, leaving his entire stay bonus on the table just as the PE company was starting to sell that company. This delayed the sale process a good eight months. After the first company was sold, the people who bought it fired this CEO, which made three jobs lost by him in only a few years.

So why do I tell you all these things?

First, when you sell a company or step down as CEO, make all your relatives leave the company. Staying does them, and you, no favors. Besides, my son ended up with a much better career position.

Second, you should either leave, or if you have to stay on the board as I had to, you should distance yourself as far from the company as possible, physically, socially, and emotionally. At first I tried to stay involved. Do as I say, not as I did.

I once met a guy who sold a prominent company when it had reached $1 billion in sales. The new owners placed him on the board. One of the first things that happened was that the new CEO decided to paint some offices red. The old guy was horrified, telling the CEO, "How could you paint *my* offices such an awful color?" The lesson he learned and tried to impart to me was to never, never, serve on the board of a company you have sold, if at all possible. And remember, that there are only two roles for a board member: (1) support the president, and (2) replace the president.

Some Generalizations about the Private Equity Industry

Generalizations can be dangerous, but, while there are exceptions, I think most of what is contained in this chapter is true and worth watching out for with any private equity company. And you will be exposed to private equity, even if you sell to a strategic buyer.

The first reason the private equity industry in America exists is because of a construct known as *carried interest*. This means that private equity companies get to treat their income, for tax purposes, as if it were capital gains. At the time of writing, the capital gains tax rate is about half of the ordinary income tax rate. Congress periodically makes moves to eliminate carried interest or to eliminate the capital gains rate entirely.

Private equity is also an "alternative" investment, or an alternative to stocks and bonds. It is very popular for institutional investing by such groups as university retirement funds for several reasons. Most significantly, returns have, in general, been higher than stocks or bonds. However, investments aren't liquid and must be held for a number of years, and the minimum commitment is often a few million dollars. Because of this, PE is often not a good investment for individuals.

How PE works: The PE firm announces a new fund. Based on its prior success or the prior success of its partners at other firms, the PE firm asks institutions to commit a sum of money, and when it obtains sufficient commitments, it goes out and buys companies. Each time it buys one, it asks the member institutions to fork over their pro-rata share of the price. So, for the first few years, the investors are contributing money.

The PE company loads up the companies it buys with lots of debt, which it pays off in five years or so. If the PE company guesses correctly, though, the debt gets paid off and the return is multiplied. And that's the second reason that the private equity industry exists. Here's an example: Suppose a PE company buys a company for $10 million. It borrows $6 million, pays it off in five or six years, and then sells the company. If the value has increased several percentage points per year, its gets about $11.5 million for only putting up $4 million. Try that with some other investments.

A PE company tries to get yet more money upon selling the company it owns by improving margins, generally by reducing costs. It seems to be an article of faith in the PE industry that most privately held companies (such as yours and mine!) are not really competently managed and that money can be squeezed out of them.

After most of the debt is paid off, the PE company sells the companies in its fund. It almost never keeps them, because much of their value comes from paying off the debt, which has now been accomplished. It almost never transfers them to its next fund, either, because the transfer value would cause a conflict between the shareholders in the old fund and the new one.

The guys you will deal with in PE will be some of the smartest people you have ever met. However, their smarts may be one-dimensional. They know a lot about finance. They are very good at reading and analyzing charts and data but not as good at walking around, talking with employees, and leading or motivating people. Some of them will lay off people just to make a quarterly or even monthly forecast, forgetting that it will be far more expensive to hire equivalent people back next quarter and will hurt morale. Morale doesn't show up on PowerPoint charts.

Sales management and product innovation often don't show up on PE guys' radar either, even though these factors may be responsible for the company's success. PE people tend to have very few actual management skills, which is why they want to buy companies with good management teams in place. They also tend to hire a lot of consultants, even if they don't need them. Sometimes this is a good thing. Other times they apply buzzwords and Japanese techniques where they're not applicable. One of your tasks may be to deflect the suggestions of your new owners and their consultants where the suggestions are not appropriate.

Many of the personality types that start and build companies are not compatible with the PE industry. I was lucky, I suppose, to have a PE company whose leader had actually worked as a manager in an industrial firm.

Private equity is a good career for kids with MBAs in finance from top schools who want to get rich. Provided they have the brains and the stomach for it, they can make a lot of money fast. For one thing, carried interest provides a lot of money. For another, their business is structured so that they're the general partners and the investors are the limited partners. That means the PE people are usually guaranteed a certain minimum return, get paid off before the limited partners, and get management fees to boot.

As a general rule, the general partners get 20 percent of the profits plus 2 percent of the assets as their fee.

Private equity is also growing in the United States, at the expense of IPOs (going public). The Sarbanes-Oxley Law has created massive amounts of paperwork for any public company without doing anybody much good, including the public it was supposed to protect. I have asked CEOs of $100-million companies and $4-billion companies what their cost of compliance with Sarbanes-Oxley is. The answers seem to center around $4 million per year. All this paperwork makes IPOs less attractive unless a firm is very large, and thus private equity is usually a more logical alternative.

No Generalizations about Strategic Buyers

Strategic buyers are a different breed. They intend to keep your company permanently, so you'll get no second bite of the apple. They also have their own management philosophies and will impose them on you to a greater or lesser extent, unlike most PE companies. So your experiences will vary.

In one example, I knew of a company whose president was told by the new owners that he had to increase earnings 15 percent every year. If not, he got fired. So the first two guys got fired. The third president got a list of all the employees, sorted by compensation, and fired all the highest paid people. Costs went down and profits went up—for a few months. Then, all those highly paid people went to work for a competitor. They knew all of the firm's customers, pricing, and so on. Profits of their former company soon plummeted. The company was sold to another strategic buyer for a fraction of its recent purchase price. The new owners, incidentally, bothered the new (fourth) president very little. They visited him once a year and, presumably, read the periodic reports he sent. Of course he was doing better than his predecessors.

A friend of mine ran a plant, one of four, for a subsidiary of a large company. He was promoted to run the whole subsidiary company and moved to the headquarters plant. Shortly after that, the company told him they were strapped for cash, had to sell something, and had chosen his subsidiary as the thing to sell because it had more value than the rest of the company. He helped to sell it to a strategic buyer, but with apprehension, fearing that the buyer might have a bench full of managers and might replace him.

After six months he had met all his objectives for the new owners and even had figured out how to consolidate production in such a way that they could eliminate one of the plants. His new bosses had indicated nothing but pleasure with his performance. He invited his boss to visit and tour the plant he had figured out how to close.

But as soon as the boss arrived in his office, my friend was told he had five minutes to clear out of the company and was handed an envelope containing his severance terms. He hired a lawyer to negotiate these terms somewhat, but as far as I know, he never did find out why he had been let go.

Then there was the owner-entrepreneur who sold his instrumentation company to a large electrical manufacturer. After that, he spent a lot of the parent company's money developing a line of new products. These absorbed a lot of cash, and profits suffered, at which point he bought the company back from the parent and created a lot of growth by selling the new products. Nice work if you can pull it off.

He eventually sold out to a big conglomerate and ended up running a group of divisions for the conglomerate.

So here's the takeaway: If you sell your company to a strategic buyer, regardless of any promises or stock options, regard the money you get on the day of closing as the last you're going to get. If you get more, it's gravy. Don't count on it.

Come to think of it, the same advice applies to a sale to a PE company. The difference is that the PE company will *usually* grant you more independence provided you're making money for them. If you're profitable, seldom will a PE company do any of the of the following to you, though I've seen strategic buyers do all of them to acquisitions in the last twelve months:

1. Get rid of your sales reps because some of the other products they represent compete with some of the parent's products—and then complain when sales go down.

2. Force you to convert to their MIS system without providing adequate support. In the case I'm thinking of, the system was down for over a month. The employees couldn't even tell the purpose of incoming material on their shipping dock. (Such things do wonders for profits!)

3. Impose their own credit terms that are inappropriate for your customers and alienate some of your customers.

4. Impose their own version of strategic pricing, being very inflexible about it and alienating other customers.

5. Decide that a certain percentage of your products could be better assembled in their plant in Mexico, erasing quality for a year or two.

6. "Save money" by eliminating your customer service team, which was a key differentiator between you and your competitors and which was responsible (though you could not prove it with charts) for giving you business, in some cases, at 5 to 10 percent higher prices.

Item 3 is more insidious than it might seem. In one case the acquired company had effective credit management by a single clerk. The company had terms of net thirty days. Big customers imposed terms such as "we'll pay you in ninety days—take it or leave it." So the vendor made minor product changes, changed the part number, and raised the price. The engineers at the customer company specified the "new" product. Their purchasing people paid the higher price in ninety days, unwittingly paying interest, and everyone was happy. But the company that acquired the small company centralized credit at their headquarters to "save money." The headquarters bean counters put these customers on credit hold if payments were even one week "late." Customers' specifying engineers got angry, switched vendors to a competitor, and the competitor even hired several of the acquired company's sales staff away.

In closing this section, I'll remind you that after selling your company, you're there temporarily, no matter the stock options. Think of the cash you get on closing as the most you're going to get.

Remember too that a strategic buyer will give you no second bite of the apple. On the other hand, a strategic buyer *may* pay more to buy your company. PE companies look only at how much they think they can increase EBITDA, but strategics may also look at synergistic effects on their existing operations.

So Who Pays the Most?

People used to think that strategic buyers would pay more than financial buyers. This is true some of the time. A strategic may need certain products to fill in a hole in its offerings, and it's cheaper to pay a premium for an existing company than to create the products or markets from scratch, but such cases are not very common.

Or a certain industry might be perceived as being a super good one to get into. For example, medical records are hot right now.

But in general, it's no longer true, if it ever was, that financial firms pay less. After all, they intend to sell the company shortly, and their buyer universe includes strategic buyers as well.

Now That You're a Total Outsider

Okay, now you have no role in the company. The second bite of the apple has been paid. You're not on the board. You do not have a consulting contract. You've gone through purgatory for the PE company, or if you were really lucky, you sold to a strategic buyer and got out right away, with no years in purgatory.

There is likely to be a great emptiness now that you have little to do. Although it's hard, you must move on and not try to reconstruct past glories. For one thing, you're likely to be too old. I was in my sixties. That meant I couldn't relive my former life as king and also that probably nobody would hire me for any job I'd be willing to do.

First of all, don't try to have influence with your former company. It's okay to socialize with a few of the people there once in awhile, but don't talk about what's happening in the company now. In all probability, you don't have very many real friends in the company anyway, because you were the boss and they were subordinates. I knew one former business owner who, well into his nineties, financed an annual Christmas party for his former employees, about 115 of them. But that was an exception.

Second, you'll possibly want to invest in another business. Let this be known and you'll have all sorts of opportunities to do so. The problem with about 99 percent of these, or at least the ones that approach you, is that they want your money, not your participation. If you've gotten out of your company with your STV, you don't need money. You need something to do.

Let me digress here and talk about what to do with your STV. I think the best thing to do is to invest it with the private client group, or whatever they call it, of a large bank. Mine was—and is—invested partially with JP Morgan and partly with PNC Bank. They treat you well, come out and see you quarterly, and answer questions and requests promptly. I chose them based on the caliber of the people who would actually mange my money, and I figured that JP Morgan would never go broke. If they did, a bunch of Saudi sheiks would issue a Fatwa against them and they'd all be dead. Motivation. Some banks I turned down included Citibank, which actually had gone bankrupt. I figured if they couldn't manage their money, they couldn't manage mine, though the private client monies hadn't been affected by their bankruptcy. Incidentally, I prefer "too good to fail" over "too big to fail."

I recommend you do something similar with your STV. From time to time other very good banks will approach you, but after you're set up, there isn't any good reason to change unless you really like the individuals managing your account and they go to work for a different bank, which happens.

Leave your STV amount with these guys. You can consider anything *in addition to* your STV as play money, but don't touch the STV. As Warren Buffet said, "The first rule is don't lose the money. The second rule is to remember the first rule."

The only problem with this strategy is that it's boring. But I can't complain because each year for the last five or six, my investment accounts have appreciated more than I can figure out how to spend. Of course, that's what they're supposed to do.

End of digression. You're probably bored and need something to do. You've had a lot of hobbies, though not much time to spend on them, but maybe not a lot of close friends, either because your coworkers thought you were the boss or you didn't have time very much for outside activities. You get approached with investment opportunities like some of these:

1. A successful fast-food chain wants to open in your town. A fund has been set up to finance ten of them. You can invest $100,000, be guaranteed to earn at least 8 percent, cash out when the fund sells in ten years, and get first dibs on the second fund then. Analysis: Who cares? I'll be in my seventies then.

2. A doctor with six degrees has invented a device and hooked up with a serial entrepreneur who is a friend of yours. The benefit of this product seems substantial compared to its cost. You can get in for $25,000. Analysis: I did. Due to so some unknown unknowns, I have lost out so far.

3. JP Morgan has started a private private-equity company for their clients. Lots of good co-investors, like Blackstone Capital and KKR. The problem, again, is all you do is give them money and wait. In ten years you'll almost certainly get a good return. Analysis: It was JP Morgan and how could I lose? I invested a small portion of my assets.

4. A bunch of guys started a fund ten years ago to buy distressed real estate in Boston. After ten years, they made a lot of money. Now they're starting Fund II and you can get in on it. Analysis: Why bother, in light of other opportunities?

5. A small (twenty-employee) software company has started up. The CEO wants you to invest money but also serve as COO. You will not get paid cash for being COO but will get paid in stock. You find many things that you could do to help them. But it turns out that a major investor who put in $2 million five years ago with little hope of getting out doesn't back up the CEO and will not let you in without investing a lot of money. Analysis: I walked away and two years later the company was liquidated.

After a few more of these, I made a hard-and-fast rule: whenever I'm approached with a business venture, I say that I'm only interested in propositions that let me own 51 percent of the stock or that are 100 percent liquid. I didn't want money. I wanted challenge. This brings up the next subject.

Owning a Second Business

The problem is, what should a second business be? I decided to explore the commercial real estate business. Through networking I found a very good commercial real estate salesman who showed me around some office buildings in my suburb. What I learned was (a) that every office building was only partially occupied; (b) every one of them was for sale; and (c) this was a boring business. Most of what you do is buy some properties and wait around for the real estate prices to increase. If the past is any guide, here in the Rust Belt, you're talking about waiting decades.

Then I thought about buying an existing business that actually made things. I recalled that at my old business, I had acquired a company that had forty-five employees and a sixty-year-old boss who wanted to stay for five years. The business was large enough to have sales, manufacturing, and other managers. The owner was competent. Instead of running it fifty-five hours a week, all my company had to do was have a weekly conference call and receive monthly financial reports. Every couple of months we visited back and forth. We paid about $6 million for this business, including all the legal and accounting acquisition costs. That was the kind of deal I wanted now.

Well, good luck. It's very hard to find any sort of decent business for sale. Most of them have been run into the ground. Unless you want to be a salesman most of your time, you're out of luck. I wanted a business large enough to have a manager and department managers, since at my age I had no desire to work fifty-five hours a week again. I made a very flexible list of my requirements and gave it to all of the business brokers I could find. Most of them never called back, even after entertaining me. The ones who did call seemed to apply the theory of "throw all the garbage on the wall and see if anything sticks." What I learned is that if you want to buy a viable business, you'd better spend about fifty-five hours a week networking, maybe for several years.

Eventually I volunteered to be a judge for the Ernst and Young Entrepreneur of the Year competition. Two years earlier I had won the regional award in the Technology category. This time, I learned that one of the judges owned a business he was trying to get rid of. Though small, it was profitable. I thought I could buy it with my son's trust fund so that there would later be no inheritance taxes, and my son could run it and use me as an unpaid consultant if he needed one. Everything looked good, except we calculated that the money my son could take out was the same as his current salary. Absent growth, there was little point in owning the business. And while it was in a stable niche, we couldn't see how to grow it.

Here are the "business" options I eventually considered. You will have similar ones in your area:

Nonprofit Boards of Directors (or Advisory Boards)

I ended up on three corporate boards, counting my old company's, and three nonprofit boards. The two types are as different as day and night.

As a general rule, nonprofit boards could care less what you know or if you know anything. Most 501(c)3 organizations try to have fifty or sixty people on their boards of trustees, which means the body is totally unworkable. But that doesn't matter to them. What matters is that the board members will give them money. A lot of a nonprofit's money comes from grants from foundations and the like, and the foundations like to hear that 100 percent of the board members have given money that year and that each trustee gave a certain amount. The "certain amount" effectively is dues you must pay for the purpose of attending four board meetings each year and maybe some committee meetings.

For example, these are the "dues" for board membership; at some institutions: $25,000 for the Cleveland Symphony Orchestra, $15,000 for the Cleveland Play House, $7,500 for the Great Lakes Science Center, and $5,000 for the Cleveland Museum of Natural History. I was on one of these boards, though the nonprofit didn't impose the mandatory dues until after I had joined.

Of course, the way these are set up, you personally don't have to donate all the money. Instead, your company can donate some of it. But I was retired and didn't have a company. Some members of these boards can justify the cost by the contacts they make. For instance, the membership of one board I was on included the CEO of a major league baseball team, the head of our largest local bank, powerful lawyers, and a partner in a large private equity firm. But I didn't have any need for such contacts. So I left this board.

Smaller nonprofits are a better choice. Their dues requirements aren't so high or so rigid. They appreciate your expertise at meetings. I joined the boards of a hospital for elderly people and a boys' boarding school.

In hindsight, I think this nonprofit board thing only works if you have some interest in the organization's activities and appreciate its mission anyway. My mother had been a patient at the hospital, and I considered it to be a loving and caring organization. My two sons had attended the boys' school.

Churches

A modification of the nonprofit-board idea is your church. You can really do some good here. You probably know more about the business aspects than the other members. Especially if the church is building an addition or planning a similar project, you can provide a lot of help while testing your ability to lead people who are not too sharp when it comes to business or finance.

I was president of the church council of a church with 1,700 members about 20 years before I sold my company. Unfortunately, I learned a lot about how stuff gets done in the church and its parent body and not much about the religion it preaches. I kind of dropped out and have not attended church regularly since then, which meant that this opportunity for involvement wasn't open to me. If it's open to you, consider taking it.

Company Boards

With a little self-promotion, you can probably get on a couple of company boards. You even get paid for it. My boards paid from $2,500 to $20,000 each year. These usually send out an agenda and performance data before each meeting, and if you spend some time reading and analyzing these materials, you can make a contribution to the company. This is fun. The only problem is that with at least four meetings each year and my seats on nonprofit boards, some meeting always seems to interfere with my vacation plans!

Keeping Your Sanity

==

I eventually realized that all this activity in support of boards was really just an attempt to reestablish my business position in the world. The same was true for my attempts to buy a company. I basically gave up on these aims because I had so little success. Like most CEO–business owners, I had too much of my self-image invested in my business. This made it hard to let go to explore other avenues of life for the next twenty-five years. In fact, it was hard to even think about myself as separate from my former business.

What Are You Good At?

To avoid malaise as much as possible, you should *write down* a list of activities that you either enjoy or would like to try if you have time after your working career is finished. I originally wrote the following three years before selling my company and eight years before my involvement with it ended:

I Would Enjoy ...

1. Hunting more, such as in Africa.

2. Learning how to fly-fish. Join a fly-fishing club.

3. Becoming a better target shooter and entering more matches.

4. Traveling more—Civil War sites, eastern Canada, Germany, the West.

5. Giving talks:

    a. Astronomy meetings
    b. Civil War roundtable

6. Oil painting.

7. Owning a second or other residence, possibly two homes, one in the Blue Ridge Mountains of Virginia and one on the Eastern Shore in Maryland.

8. Eating out at a good restaurant twice per week.

9. Writing articles about firearms and other topics.

10. Teaching a course or two—CWRU adult program, CCC, BW, maybe JCU (all local colleges).

11. Writing my autobiography.

12. Writing novels.

13. Consulting, if I knew how to get into it.

Three years later, I wrote down these choices:

1. Work for someone (my company's new owners?)

2. Teach (university courses or adult education?)

3. Write?

4. Paint?

5. Volunteer for something?

6. Bum around?

7. Lobby for causes (NFIB, Buckeye Institute?)

8. Get a job as a CEO for some little company?

9. Buy some small business and run it with my sons?

10. Run some one-man business that makes just enough to pay the rent on an office?

So what happened?

Starting with the original list I saw three years later that I still had a desire to work, and I did so for the new owners, with the results already described. I also explored being an adjunct professor. Teaching one course a semester only paid $3,600 and since courses met each week, I couldn't go away on vacation. Enough said.

I've always liked to write and have written a lot since retirement. As yet I've not done any oil painting. Then there's volunteering, but for what? Lobbying for some cause I believed in sounded good. I tried to find a small company to run, but I'm not sure how hard I tried. Ditto for buying one.

As for the longer list, I have always liked hunting, and I've now been big game hunting in Africa three times, but I haven't tried fly-fishing yet, although I took a course in it. Item 3 refers to my history as the junior rifle-shooting champion of Ohio. I did shoot more, but I'm too old to be very good at matches. My wife and I have travelled a lot, and I've given some talks at the local astronomy club. We bought a condo overlooking the Chesapeake Bay, and yes, we eat out a lot. I wrote two magazine articles that were accepted for publication, but the magazine went out of business before printing the second one.

I already discussed why I didn't pursue teaching. Instead of novels, I'm writing this book and am finishing an autobiography for my descendants. I wrote a short book about my three week trip to a remote corner of Zimbabwe, and that gave me an immense sense of achievement, so I'm writing this book.

Finally, I decided I really didn't want to be a consultant. There's just too much selling involved. One thing about having your STV in hand is that you get to do what you want to do.

And oh yes, we have season tickets to the Symphony and to two series of plays. Cleveland has one of the top five symphony orchestras in the world and the second largest playhouse district in North America.

So I guess that's a good start. Make your own list and then pursue the items on it. The problem is that all of those things are basically hobbies, and it's sometimes hard for a driven executive type to gain fulfillment from hobbies, no matter how well done. There is always the desire to reprise one's business career. As Lee Iacocca said, that's how you fail retirement.

I think a lot of retired people spend time with their hobbies. My father-in-law retired with a pension and played golf almost every day for twenty-five years. Unfortunately, most of us who have built businesses aren't wired for leisure. High achievers seem to need purpose and goals.

You may also fear losing your self-worth. You just have to get over it. I've spent a lot of time on the activities mentioned here. For instance, I was president of the Cuyahoga Astronomy Association in 1987. Later I basically dropped out. I have now returned and found some fascinating people, and I have reestablished a circle of friends there and elsewhere. They are not high-pressure people. One problem was that I had few friends before. I worked too many hours to make real friendships and spent most of my time with employees, who are never really friends. Now I feel I've adjusted. It takes a couple of years. Just don't try to rebuild your business career from the past forty years in the next two years.

After awhile, it won't seem useless to drive your grandchildren to school or art lessons.

If I get time, I'll check out that fly-fishing club.

Setting Up Your Legacy

Another problem that most people don't really have to think about is what to do with their money for their heirs. If you have your STV or more, you do have to worry about this. There are several theories on what to do with your money. Some people worry that their children or grandchildren will not be responsible stewards. My belief is that however irresponsible they may become, my heirs will be much more responsible in managing or spending my assets than the US government has been. So I want my money funneled to them, not the government.

When I was still working, my attorney recommended I set up a dynasty trust for each of my two sons. This is a trust that hopefully grows for four hundred years, benefitting them and their descendants. It is immune from inheritance taxes. The trustee (whom they are allowed to change, since I might not live to be four hundred) will pay them funds for housing, education, or medical expenses. Later, I came to not favor this kind of trust. For one thing, beyond my grandchildren, I don't much empathize with descendants for the next four hundred years. For another, my two sons already have obtained houses, jobs, and medical plans and have completed their educations. I've also already funded the grandchildren's college educations with 529 plans.

Far better trusts for my purposes are the ones I set up to buy my mother's shares of stock in the company. As a result, upon sale of the firm, my sons own more than they or my mother ever paid in.

Finally, in 2012 my wife and I set up a "pot" trust for our grandchildren. The way that worked, after about ten years, the trust splits up into individual trusts for each then-living grandchild.

This sounds complicated, but the result is that my children and grandchildren will want for nothing, including education expenses (as noted, we have 529 funds for the grandchildren) and mortgage payments for their lifetimes.

Having given away considerable money already, my wife and I are left with more than our required STV. The rest is available for some business proposition, should one arise, or for charitable contributions. The STV should survive us and be made available to our heirs or, should we choose, become a charitable bequest, in whole or in part.

Right now I'm having one of the groups that invests my money perform a calculation that will show whether I could ever run out of money given certain investments and ambitions at certain times in the future. That's a fancy way of saying that my STV may become more than I need based on any reasonable life expectancy. I anticipate that about ten years from now, armed with this calculation and having greater comfort about my assets, my wife and I may increase our charitable donations.

The important way to think about your legacy is to think of it as four separate pots that you will not mix:

1. Your secure threshold value (STV). This is your security.

2. Trust funds or other provisions you make for your children or grandchildren. The amounts and forms are your choice.

3. Money for charitable contributions.

4. Your play money. This is the only pot with which you will gamble or take a flier on a business venture.

Even if you divide your money this way, it is best to maintain a low-beta lifestyle: be conservative in life and business at this stage. But if you remember how much is in each pot and keep the pots separate, this won't matter as much.

Keeping Your Soul Intact

No matter what you do or how you think, you will conclude that the people who end up running your company are dunderheads. They will not be as committed as you were. They will not care a whit about employees who may have worked for you long term, even at salaries a bit lower than they could get elsewhere, and their idea of loyalty can best be expressed as WIIFM—what's in it for me?

They will make many mistakes that will hurt the employees, lower morale, and cost the company money. But they may also do some things that will grow the company, including doing some things better than you did.

Some of the things that caused me anguish:

1. Firing the manufacturing guy who had been with the company for twenty-five years.

2. Random layoffs to meet numbers, which destroyed the cooperative culture of the company without replacing it with anything of value.

3. Evening out shipment statistics by arbitrarily delaying shipments, even when they had been promised to customers for a certain date.

4. Trying to save money by simply not paying bonuses that people had been accustomed to getting.

5. My passing on Emails from customers (who thought I was still CEO) complaining about something or asking for a quote that often received no follow-up.

6. Abolishing our employee profit-sharing plan.

When I mentioned these things, the head of the PE group told me to not bring them up and not to say anything in the board meetings that might embarrass the new CEO. Well, I was getting paid to go to board meetings. Moreover, I had some stock options that only fully vested after five years or if the PE firm sold the company. I didn't want to walk away from these, and eventually they paid me a lot of money. So I sat down and shut up.

How do you avoid things like this happening to you?

The best way is to have nothing to do with the company after you sell it. But if you have a contract or options that vest after several years, you can't avoid this. So have as little to do with the board as possible. Consider that you only have one of two purposes on the board: to support the president or to recommend that the president be fired.

And throw yourself into some other activities.

A Mistake: Feeling That You Have an Obligation to Protect the Employees

As I watched the new regime destroy the culture of the company without replacing it with something better or even understanding the need to do this, I felt an obligation to protect long-term employees. During my one-year consulting contract that started one year after I left as president, I arranged to have an office at one of the company's buildings. Bad mistake. Whenever I used it, disgruntled employees would come up and tell me how things were getting screwed up. Eventually I stopped using this office.

A number of employees got fired unfairly, which also demotivated the remaining employees. Whenever some of these asked, I would write recommendations for them on LinkedIn. I helped some others get jobs through networking. I considered the employees almost as friends. The trouble was that they considered me boss, perhaps a fair boss but a boss nevertheless. With rare exceptions, few of them ever thanked me for my efforts on their behalf.

So my advice is to let the employees take care of their own situations. Write a recommendation if asked, but that's all. Don't agonize over the unfairness of it all.

I always ran my business as if we really cared for the people we employed, because we did. It was capitalism with a human face. That very concept would elicit a frown of disbelief from many private equity partners and from most employees of strategic buyers as well. So run your company that way while you're still running it, but when it's over, it's over. Don't anguish over that.

Keep repeating, "Do not regret the past."

I did the best I could for myself and for my family, although there is possibly one new way to do things …

A Better Way?

Any exit you create will almost certainly result in some dismemberment of the company you built. PE companies will flip it every few years or strategic buyers will dismantle it, perhaps inadvertently. A friend of mine thought up a different strategy, which probably applies only to certain situations but is definitely worth considering.

My friend owns a company that his father founded in the 1950s. Forty years ago, when it had eight employees, my friend was persuaded to join the family firm. The company designed and manufactured a type of testing machine for which vendor service and quality were important. At the time, he was working for a big bank. He was in a rat race with all of his associates. The reward was that he would get to run in a bigger rat race if he stayed at the bank. His father persuaded him to at least try the family business. He would get experience in sales, accounting, purchasing, and a little engineering and would at least have a useful resume if he didn't like it.

He did like it. Over the next forty years, the company grew to 180 employees and became the world leader in its small but important niche. My friend's children both had good careers and had no interest in running the company, so fifteen years ago, my friend began planning his unique exit strategy. Like most of us, my friend did not want to see his life's work or his employees devoured in the maw of financiers.

As he explains it, "My objective is the continuation and preservation of this company as an independent and vibrant organization. It serves a valuable economic and social purpose. It deserves to continue to operate according to the same values we have followed for the past fifty-seven years. I don't want to see it bought by a private equity group or a strategic buyer and then get sucked into the quarterly earnings rat race. That would be the destruction of my life's work."

So here is the approach he took:

The Trust

First, he established a *perpetual* trust, which will be a taxable entity, not a charity. The laws in this state (Ohio) permit this. The purpose of the trust, in his exact words, is "to advance the art of manufacturing, with special emphasis on materials testing. The trust will pursue its mission by owning and operating manufacturing companies that embody the highest principles of manufacturing excellence, free enterprise, ethical dealing, and creation of value for customers. Its success at its stated purpose will be evaluated by societal value added, essentially the same as profit."

Eventually this trust will own most of his company, up to 99 percent; it and may acquire other companies in the future; and the major beneficiary of the trust will be the company itself. The reason for the 99 percent is to avoid "circular references" under Ohio law. Other beneficiaries could include family members and charities.

Ownership Transfer Process

Since the company is a subchapter S company, it has undistributed earnings. In fact, these may be most of its value. These earnings will be transferred to my friend and will exceed his STV. Note that there are no taxes due on such a transfer because they have already been paid. This will net him a lot of money, more than he thinks he could ever spend in retirement. Also, he owns the company's real estate and will continue leasing it to the company.

After the trust is set up, the company will be recapitalized with two classes of stock, voting and nonvoting. The nonvoting stock will have most of the value. My friend will own the voting stock, and the nonvoting stock will be sold to the trust. To enable the trust to get a bank loan, my friend will probably have to contribute about $200,000 of cash to it.

And that's basically that! Check with your own legal advisors if you want to emulate this strategy. At my friend's death, the corporation/trust will not have to pay large inheritance taxes. My friend's estate might. The laws in your state may vary.

In my opinion, it will work because of (a) the large amount of undistributed earnings in the sub-S corporation right now; (b) the fact that the company has no debt; and (c) the fact that my friend's children have their own careers and do not want to manage the company. All things considered, my friend thinks that he and his heirs will net perhaps 10 or 15 percent less than they would have with an outright sale to "short-term thinkers," as he calls them.

He thinks this is well worth it. So do I.

My friend is going to gradually leave the picture. He has hired managers he thinks can be successors. The biggest problem, he thinks, is how to ensure that after his death successor trustees and directors follow the mission. This will become clearer as the trust agreement is written and finalized. Is it impossible? Milton Hershey's candy company has been owned by a charitable trust since 1905.

But the point is that he has found what may be a better way to exit his company than those the hordes of advisors recommend. He is having his cake and eating it too.

And he's going to take it with him!

At a recent meeting, he told all his employees that he was working on a succession plan that would allow the company to continue without selling it to the Wall Street guys. The applause was very loud!

Some Takeaways

1. You can't avoid an exit strategy. You already have one. It's called surprise death. Pick a better one.

2. Make your plan about five years—or fifteen—before you need to do it. You can change your plan, but you can't plan too far ahead.

3. You will not help your family, your business, or your employees by working fifty-five hours a week until you collapse on your desk at age eighty-five.

4. Guess what? You don't own your business. Your business owns you. Unlike Jack Welch, the pope, the janitor, or ordinary mortals, you can't just quit. It's a process.

5. Think of how long it will take you to exit once you push the Start button, and then plan on it taking twice as long.

6. Likewise, plan for the exit to take about eight times as much work as you think it will.

7. Set aside emotions before you start planning. Your business is not a member of your family. Forget the past. The future is important.

8. If you run a family business, your legacy is your kids and grandkids, not your distant ancestors or more distant descendants.

9. Hire the best mergers-and-acquisitions lawyers and investment bankers you can find. And then verify everything they do.

10. Network. Talk to everyone you meet who is at all involved in running or selling a company. Join Vistage and bring your concerns to your group.

11. Be absolutely truthful during due diligence and the rest of the sale process.

12. Don't flunk retirement. Long in advance, figure out something, you're going to do to occupy your time and maximize your creativity.

13. Enjoy yourself. It's later than you think.

14. Always recognize which of the five stages of business yours is in.

15. If you leave your company, make sure all your relatives leave too. If your replacement is insecure, he or she will want them gone.

16. Distance yourself from the company as far as possible. If possible, do not run it very long for the new owners, serve on the board, or have other involvement, though you will possibly have to do these things for a few years.